Martial Arts™

the
Kung Fu
handbook

Martial Arts™

the

Kung Fu handbook

Peter Warr

ROSEN PUBLISHING®

New York

This North American edition published in 2008 by:

The Rosen Publishing Group, Inc.
29 E. 21st Street
New York, NY 10010

North American edition, this format, printed in 2008
by The Rosen Publishing Group, Inc.

Copyright © 2004 by D&S Books Ltd.

Creative Director: Sarah King
Project Editor: Anna Southgate
Photographer: Colin Bowling
Designer: Axis Design Editions

Library of Congress Cataloging-in-Publication Data

Warr, Peter G.
The kung fu handbook / Peter Warr. — North
American ed.
    p. cm. — (Martial arts)
Includes bibliographical references and index.

ISBN-13: 978-1-4042-1392-0 (library binding)
1. Kung fu—Handbooks, manuals, etc.—Juvenile
literature. I. Title.
GV1114.7.W37 2008
796.815'9—dc22

2007035824

Manufactured in China

contents

introduction

In writing a book for the beginner on Chinese martial arts, it is quite easy to fall into the trap of using Chinese phrases, physiological terminology and other technical jargon. Such an approach may be impressive but, quite often, it can be confusing to the reader. Another trap is that of oversimplification. This may make for an easier read, but unfortunately essential information gets discarded. Both of these approaches are unhelpful and confusing.

Instead, I have tried to achieve a happy medium. I have used English translations as far as possible, but have included the Chinese terms as points of reference. I have also included the physiological information where it is appropriate, although it is not essential in understanding the main body of text.

As I mention above, this book is for the beginner, or for those who have been training for just a short while. It will cover the various aspects of training in Kung Fu as well as giving the reader an idea of what Kung Fu is about.

The correct term for Chinese martial arts is Wushu, the translation of Wu means "military/martial" and Shu means "art." Kung Fu is a term, which comes from Hong Kong, the translation of which is: "a man who is skilled with his hands."

There are many different, and differing, styles of Kung Fu/Wushu. Some of these you will find in the later chapters of this book. However, all styles of Kung Fu/Wushu share some elemental components, and it is on these that I have focused in the first half of this book. In the second half of the book I have focused on how these elemental components are integrated into two specific, and ultimately very different, styles of Kung Fu/Wushu.

Remember: As with all exercises you must only train to a level that is comfortable for you. If you have a health problem or injury, please consult you doctor before doing any form of training, whether it is in martial arts, or for running or using fitness machines.

Thank you for choosing this book, I hope you enjoy it. Peter Warr, 2004.

Countering a punch with an elbow strike to the ribs in Bow Stance posture.

the history of chinese
chapter 1 martial arts (kung fu/wushu)

The history goes back to primitive times, when tribes roamed the vast country of China. Their fight wasn't for trophies or medals, but for survival against wild animals and other tribes or even within their own hierarchy (pecking order).

Martial arts began as a form of wrestling, imitating wild beasts. Participants would intertwine their arms to mimic the interlocking horns of animals and the stronger would try and subdue the weaker.

The only weapons that would have been available at this time would have been primitive clubs, sticks and small rocks.

As the tribes became more organized so too did their combat skills and through inter-tribal warfare they started to develop more sophisticated weapons. They sharpened the ends of sticks to make what are known today as spears. By tying a shaped rock to a club, they produced a weapon that we would recognize today as an axe.

There were also tribal dances used for festivals or to prepare for war, where the actions of animals proved a great source of inspiration: for example "the courtship dance of the strutting peacock" or "the war-like stamping and chest beating of the great ape." Furthermore there are many ancient stories in Chinese mythology, where one creature comes to blows against another, such as a crane attacking a snake and an eagle attacking a bear.

It is one theory that the Chinese tribes took inspiration from the dances and mythology in honing their combat skills.

shang period (16–11 century BCE)

As tribal society developed so, too, did their combat skills. The most dramatic change came during the Bronze Age in China between the (16th and 11th centuries BCE).

With the use of bronze there was a huge advancement in the development of weapons, such as the battle-axe, the halberd, spear, straight sword, bow and arrow and the broadsword.

The tribal societies had by this time formed organized armies, which were well equipped with horses, armor and long-handled weapons like the long-handled broadsword (gwando).

Horsemanship skills improved in order to use the weapons more effectively.

spring & autumn and warring states period (770–220 BCE)

During this period armed and unarmed combat skills became highly developed, with many methods of attack, defense and counterattack.

Martial art competitions became very popular and, owing to a lack of protective clothing, many people were seriously wounded or killed. This did not stop the enthusiasm for competing, however.

Sword fighting became very popular around this time and many of the competitors were left with badly scarred faces and bodies.

The love of sword fighting was shared by women as well as men.

qin dynasty (221–207 BCE)

Competitions became much more strict during this period, with the enforcement of rules, the placement of referees and the development of the laitai (a raised open ring; pronounced lay tie). So you had not only the skill of combat but also the skill of having to stay on the laitai.

During the periods previously mentioned, combat skills had been used to train the armies whose leaders who were always struggling for supremacy. Many of the famous generals at the time were very skilled in armed and unarmed combat, and by this time the martial skills were continuously being refined or modified to keep up with the developing weaponry.

With the numerous weapons now being used, the most popular were known as the Eighteen Weapons (sword, longbow, crossbow, lance, battle-axe, staff, long-blade spear, cudgel, dagger axe, fork, truncheon, mallet, jingal, jointed bludgeon, chain, hooks, halberd and shield).

han dynasty (206 BCE–220 CE) to sui tang dynasty (518–907 CE)

The development of martial arts within the military forces continued through the Han and Sui Tang Dynasties. Officers had to take examinations so they could be ranked by their skill. These examinations consisted of armed or unarmed combat, on foot or on horseback.

So now you can see how the Chinese martial arts developed through the military training. Many students in the West have only heard of the word of Kung Fu for Chinese martial arts, but in fact the correct term for all Chinese martial arts is Wushu. The term Wushu covers all aspects and styles of the Chinese martial arts.

The Chinese character Wu 武 means military.

The Chinese character for Shu 式 means art.

Therefore bringing the two characters together simply brings the military training and the arts together. Wu Shu cannot be translated directly into English, but is generally known as Chinese martial arts.

song dynasty (960–1279 CE)

During the Song Dynasty martial art associations were organized and set up in the different regions of China with the art of Kung Fu/Wushu being the most popular.

A section of the civilian population was now giving Kung Fu/Wushu performances at festivals.

With many street performers showing their prowess by breaking large rocks with their bare hands, breaking spear shafts (being pressed to their throat), by far the most popular performance was that of taking on any and all challengers who wished to test their own skills.

ming dynasty (1368–1644 CE)

During the Ming Dynasty, Kung Fu/Wushu started to form many different schools.

Before this time martial arts had mostly been passed down through word of mouth from Master to student; there was very little written down, as Masters kept their own techniques secret from the other schools or Masters.

However, there are drawings that have been uncarthed dating back to the primitive age, which show men wrestling (Shuai Chiao) and in different combat stances.

qing dynasty (1644–1911 CE)

During the Qing Dynasty, 1644–1911, the schools became more defined in their differing skills, each one developing its own approach to the many methods of training. There was also a rise in secret societies that used Kung Fu/Wushu to great effect.

It is said that, as students practiced their art, they were taught poems or songs, the words of which held the secret of their fighting skills. Outside that particular school, therefore, nobody would know the meaning of the song or poem.

It was during this period that many of the styles that we know of today were developed, such as Tan Tui, Xingyiquan, Taijiquan, Baghuaquan, Changquan, Bajiquan and Tongbiquan.

In 1910 the Jing Wu Sports Society (Shanghai) was formed and that was the beginning of the Kung Fu/Wushu martial arts that we know today.

In 1928 the now-famous Nanjing Academy (the Central Wushu Institute) was set up by the Chinese Government to develop Kung Fu/Wushu as a structured training syllabus, not just for self-defense but for the obvious health benefits it affords.

It was during the Qing Dynasty that many of the styles known today were developed – including Taijiquan.

Both the Jing Wu and the Nanjing's main objective was to enhance the different schools of Kung Fu/Wushu. They examined each movement and every posture in minute detail in order to identify the origins of each one. As a result, the Kung Fu/Wushu school developed into an art form, with involvement from the top Kung Fu/Wushu experts, who had many years of experience passed down through their respective families. They could correct the postures and techniques, allowing the body to harmonize through the movements.

Within the schools, through watching the students of various heights, weights and abilities practicing, experts were also able to identify the attack and defense methods and to make improvements thus making the Kung Fu/Wushu much more effective for each and every student.

These are the foundations of what we see in Kung Fu/Wushu today. It has been said that a Kung Fu/Wushu form looks like ballet with gymnastics combined.

To be a ballerina you need great strength and flexibility, while a gymnast requires tremendous agility. Combine this with the attack and defense techniques of Kung Fu/Wushu, and you have a martial art that is not only beautiful to watch but also instills discipline, virtue and skill in each and every student.

northern external kung fu schools – hard style

As Kung Fu/Wushu developed, different systems became popular within their own provinces. There are well over 100 different schools and many more individual schools within these groups. To give you some idea as to the differing styles, I have listed some of these below. Unfortunately there are just to many to list them all.

A generic term for these systems is: above the Yangtze River (Yellow River) Northern Style; Chang-Quan:

Shaolin Quan	Shaolin Boxing
Fanzi Quan	Wheeling Boxing
Zha Quan	Zha School of Boxing
Hwa Quan	Essence Boxing
Hua Quan	Flower Boxing
Pao Quan	Cannon Boxing
Hong Quan	Hong School of Boxing
Tonbi Quan	Full Arm Boxing
Mizong Quan	Maze Boxing
Liuhe	Six Harmony Boxing
Tan Tui	Spring Leg Boxing
Chuo Jiao	Jabbing Feet
Baji Quan	Eight Ultimate Boxing
Taizu Chang Quan	Great Ancestor Boxing
Mian Quan	Silk Floss Boxing

Chang-Quan

Tanglang

Northern styles are characterized by speed and strength, with an emphasis on variations of footwork techniques and high and low kicks. Hence the expression "Northern Leg."

There are other schools, those of imitation boxing; Hou Quan (Monkey Boxing), Zui Quan (Drunken Boxing), Ditang Quan (Tumbling Boxing), Tanglang (Praying Mantis Boxing). All these schools come under the generic term of "external" schools.

internal schools–soft style

Taijiquan is known as an "internal" school of Kung Fu/Wushu and has five major schools; Chen, Yang, Wu, Sun and Wu/Hao.

Chen School is the oldest known form and is a very powerful form of Taijiquan, becoming more popular in the West.

Yang Style is the most popular form of Taijiquan and was promoted by the Chinese government in the 1950s as a health exercise.

As stated above there is also the Wu, Hao and Sun styles. These styles are not so popular outside China.

Taijiquan is characterized by soft, light and slow exercise, which features continuously circling and fluent movements. The different schools of Taijiquan stresses the different aspects, hence the expression "soft" school or "internal" styles.

Taijiquan is a very powerful martial art and many of the old Masters, who have gone down in history for their prowess within the fighting arts, have used this system.

The slow, focused and concentrated movements can be developed into very powerful postures for defense or attack, bringing greater strength within the body.

Taijiquan posture.

other internal schools

Xingyiquan (Mind and Will Boxing)

Baghua Zhang (Eight Trigram Boxing)

Although the schools are listed as "hard," "external," "soft," "internal," "Northern" or "Southern," there is always a relationship between the hard and soft. This relationship is described as Yin and Yang.

Xingyiquan Posture.

The main difference between the hard and soft styles lies in their approach to the training. There are many stories of how the old Masters developed their fighting skills. One such story is how a Master watched the Crane attack the Snake. The Crane was hovering above the Snake, and looked very light with its massive wingspan holding it in flight. But the power of its beak and talons as they stabbed down at the snake epitomized the Yang element which is hard.

Meanwhile, the Snake was twisting, turning and coiling trying to evade the crane's attack, but also counterstriking with tremendous speed and accuracy. This epitomized the Yin element, which is soft.

Another story is of the Eagle and the Bear. The Eagle was very quick in attacking the Bear, swooping down with very fast and strong attacks—Yin. Meanwhile, the Bear struck out with his powerful arms—Yang.

Baghua Zhang Posture.

southern external schools–hard style

In provinces below the Yangtze River, the generic term is known as Southern style or Nanquan. Many of these schools originated in the Fujian and Guandong provinces, and much later spread throughout southern China.

Southern schools are characterized by powerful exertion of force, firm and steady footwork, clear-cut movements, strong positioning of body to react to an attack from any direction, emphasis on upper body attack and defense, hence the expression "Southern Fist."

Nanquan – forward Bow Stance and Tiger Claw.

The most popular, and known as the five great schools are:	
Hongjia Quan	Hong School of Boxing
Liujia Quan	Liu School of Boxing
Ciajia Quan	Cai School of Boxing
Lijia Quan	Li School of Boxing
Mojia Quan	Mo School of Boxing

There are many other schools:	
Huhe Shuang Xing Quan	Tiger Crane Boxing
Yong Chuan Quan	Eternal Youth Boxing
Xia Quan	Knight Boxing
Hakka Quan	Hakka Boxing
Fojia Quan	Buddhist Boxing
Baimei Quan	White Eyebrow Boxing
Ru Quan	Confucian Boxing
Nanji Quan	Southern Skills Boxing
Kunhan Quan	Kunlun Boxing
Kongmen Quan	House of Kong Boxing
Lianshou Quan	Han Boxing

Standing on one leg and tiger claw.

health benefits

It became very apparent that training in Kung Fu/Wushu had numerous health benefits. The hard style was good for the younger students and increased their fitness while enabling them to perform a range of routines.

Chinese scientists/doctors conducted extensive research into these exercises and found that they were good for increasing flexibility and stamina while helping to alleviate heart and lung conditions. It was also recognized as good for personal development and discipline in the younger generation. The internal arts like Taijiquan and Qigong were more accessible to the older generation.

If you are in China and go to the parks very early in the morning, you will find hundreds of people practicing these arts. Taijiquan has now become one of the most popular health exercises throughout the world.

There is much Western research being conducted to try and find out about the health benefits of Taijiquan. Studies so far have shown that these kinds of exercise can help relieve stress, tension, bad circulation, high blood pressure, migraines, stiffness of the joint and back pain.

Kung Fu/Wushu has always had very strong links with Traditional Chinese Medicine (TCM): looking back through time the majority of old Masters were not only Kung Fu/Wushu experts, they were also the local herbalists, acupuncturists and bonesetters. As with the martial arts, this knowledge and skill was passed down through their families.

Much of the knowledge and wisdom that has been collected over the years is being used by the big research institutes in China, with doctors and scientists examining and experimenting on how Kung Fu/Wushu postures and movements can have such a dynamic effect on the body.

There are many studies that have been carried out on lung and heart diseases, rheumatism, immobility of joints and balance. The research information is available on the Internet.

Taijiquan posture

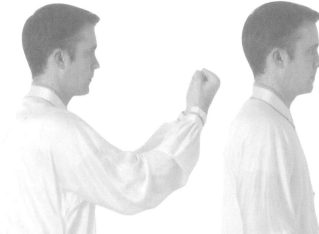

1900 onward

In 1936 Kung Fu/Wushu delegates were sent out to visit Southeast Asia in order to spread and develop the many different styles of Kung Fu. In the same year the Chinese Wushu Team gave a demonstration at the XI Olympic Games in Berlin.

Since the founding of the People's Republic of China (1949) Kung Fu/Wushu has become a component of the Chinese culture, and is on all physical education curricula. Wushu is listed in all sports institutes.

The Chinese Wushu Association was set up in 1956. The State Physical, Cultural & Sports Commission in 1958 introduced the first draft of Wushu Competition Rules, which was officially adopted that same year.

Throughout Wushu history from primitive times to today, the fundamental rationale for competitions was to spread the knowledge and skills and to enhance the development of Kung Fu/Wushu.

The term Kung Fu originated in Hong Kong and means "a working man" or "a skilled man that works with his hands." You could say that a chef's Kung Fu is good. This does not mean that he does martial arts, but that he is a good chef and that his cooking is excellent.

Kung Fu as we know it in the West, did not become popular until the early 1970s, the Bruce Lee era.

Since then there has been an explosion of Kung Fu and a steady progression of interest within the art/film world. The first television series was David Carradine's (*Kung Fu*), Jackie Chan has made numerous successful films, Chow Yun Fat is well known for *Crouching Tiger, Hidden Dragon*, and Jet Li is now the new Kung Fu star. All these high-profile images have been very good for the promotion of Kung Fu.

I can remember training during the sixties with only half dozen people in the class. By the mid seventies there was regularly over a hundred at each class, and at weekend seminars I have seen anything up to 500 students taking part. The quest for learning more about the Chinese arts still goes on today.

Even after forty years of training I have come to realize that the more I learn, the less I know. An old Chinese saying is "the ripples on a pond do not reveal its depth."

The International Wushu Federation (which is a full member of the International Olympic Committee) and the Executive & Technical Committees backed by the Chinese Sports Ministry, are all working toward Kung Fu/Wushu being entered into the 2008 Olympic Games, which will be held in Beijing.

This would be the next gigantic step in the development of Kung Fu/Wushu.

Within all major martial arts there is a strict form of etiquette, a code of training and discipline. This stems from its military foundations.

Salutation

Every school or style of martial arts has a different salutation. For example, in the Japanese and Korean arts the salutation is normally shown with a bow of the head.

In Chinese Kung Fu/Wushu the salutation is usually demonstrated by the left hand covering the knuckles of the right fist, while holding the hands at chest height, center of body. Traditional styles of Kung Fu/Wushu may have different salutations.

Whichever school of martial arts you are doing, the salutation is always performed when entering or leaving the training hall. It is also performed at the beginning and end of a class and at the beginning and end of a training/sparring session with your training partner.

The salutation shows respect toward your training hall, your instructor and/or your training partner. The significance of the right fist covered by the left palm, shows that you will not use the fist in malice, it also shows the union of Yin and Yang – soft and hard.

Within the many traditional styles, the salutation may vary and be quite different from what I have explained above, but it will still be the training code for that particular style of Kung Fu/Wushu.

The head instructor of that school would be addressed as "Sifu" (which means "teacher." In the old days when the Master only took on one or two students "Sifu" meant "second father").

clothing

You should always wear the uniform of the particular style that you are training in, and make efforts to keep yourself and your uniform clean and tidy.

Remove ALL jewelry and spectacles before you train. This is for your own safety.

Make sure that your nails are kept short and clean on both your hands and feet. This is necessary for the safety of not only yourself but your partner as well.

If your hair is long, then the hair should be tied back.

If you have or have had any medical conditions or injuries you should consult your doctor and get his/her permission, before embarking on any form of training.

Then, if you are on any medication or have any medical problems (this includes any injuries whether old or new), then you should always inform your instructor and keep him informed if the medication changes.

can I do kung fu?

This is a question I am frequently asked. It is essential to have realistic expectations, although anyone can train in Kung Fu/Wushu, it just depends on what you are looking for in a class. To achieve a high level of skill will take time and dedication.

If you are looking for just fitness or self-defense then almost any style would be okay providing it is done with safety in mind.

If you like the idea of getting into the competition side then you must choose a style/instructor that will give you the encouragement/incentive to this type of training.

However, as a potential student you should be aware that training for competition is usually very challenging, different, and much more demanding than the normal class training.

what should I look for?

Check that the style is recognized by your country's governing body and get any information that they have. This should ensure that the school/style is reputable.

In the United States, the International Wushu Federation (IWUF) is the governing body recognized by the International Olympic Committee. In other countries, information on governing bodies should be available from that country's National Sports Council/Committee.

You should always ask what qualifications the instructors have in the style that they are teaching, are they insured, and who is their teacher.

If you are able to, attend the class for an introduction session, to see whether or not you like it. However, not all classes/instructors will allow this.

Get some background information on the styles that are in your area, this may help in deciding where to go. A rule of thumb is "if you like the instructor and what he/she is teaching then stay with it, if not find somewhere else."

Discipline is also something that you should be aware of, some students may find this part challenging, but providing the instructor knows his art then all good martial arts schools will run a disciplined class/seminar.

chapter 3 **warm-up exercises**

At the beginning of every class there should be a warm-up exercise period and at the end of a class a cool-down exercise period.

Both periods are integral parts of the class, as they reduce the risk of injury. Warming up the body ensures the muscle groups are prepared to perform the required stances, punches and kicks of the martial art.

There are many different kinds of warm-up exercise, but you must be sure that each is safe for you to perform.

Your instructor will have his/her own set of exercises, and a session usually lasts about twenty minutes.

In many cases you may find that the exercises complement the martial art system that you are training in.

There should always be time for a cool-down exercise period at the end of each class, in order to allow the body to return to its natural state.

The following twelve exercises are very basic, but they do have the desired effect of warming up the body.

the exercises

As with all exercises, be aware of anything that may feel painful or uncomfortable. If any exercise affects you in this way then either reduce the size of the exercise or stop. If you get a persistent ache or pain then stop all exercises and consult your doctor.

no.1 hip rolling

This is to warm up the abdominals, the lower back muscle groups and loosen the hip joints and pelvis.

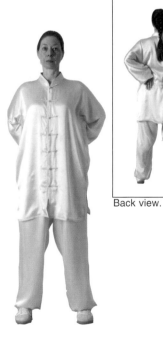

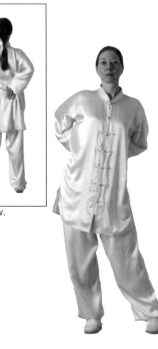

Back view.

1. Stand with your feet shoulder-width apart. Place your palms firmly on the lower back.

2. Rotate the hips one way (for eight rotations).

3. Then reverse the direction (for eight rotations).

no.2 body turns

To warm up the muscles in the upper body (latissimus dorsi, trapezius and pectoralis major).

1. Stand with your feet shoulder-width apart. Bring your arms up to shoulder level with the palms facing down.

2. Turn your body to the left and then to the right.

3. Your eyes should follow your hands as you turn. Keep your body relaxed but upright. Turn eight times on each side.

no.3 side stretch

To warm up the latissimus dorsi and external oblique muscles.

1. Stand with your feet shoulder-width apart. Stretch the left arm upward above your head with the palm facing up. Place your right palm on your right hip. Stretch over to your right, eight times, and repeat on the opposite side.

2. To increase the stretch, slide the right palm down your thigh, maintaining the stretch on the left side.

Repeat this movement eight times on each side.

no.4 wrist & ankle rolling

This exercise is to loosen up the ulna and radius joints in the arm along with the carpals in the hand. In the leg, the fibula joints and the tarsals are loosened. This particular exercise is very good for circulation.

Standing comfortably, intertwine the fingers and circle the hands. With all your weight on one leg, raise your other foot onto the toes and circle your foot.

This exercise is done on both sides, and you may find one side is easier to do than the other.

no.5 shoulder rotations

The muscles used in this exercise are the pectorals and deltoids. It also works the rib cage.

1. Stand with feet shoulder-width apart. Place your fingertips on your collarbone.

2. Circle your elbows down, then backward and forward. (Make sure this is as big a rotation as is comfortable for you).

3. Reverse the rotation. Circle the shoulders eight times forward then eight times back.

If you notice any discomfort make the rotations smaller or stop altogether.

no.6 neck rolling

The muscles used in this exercise are the sternocleidomastoid and trapezius.

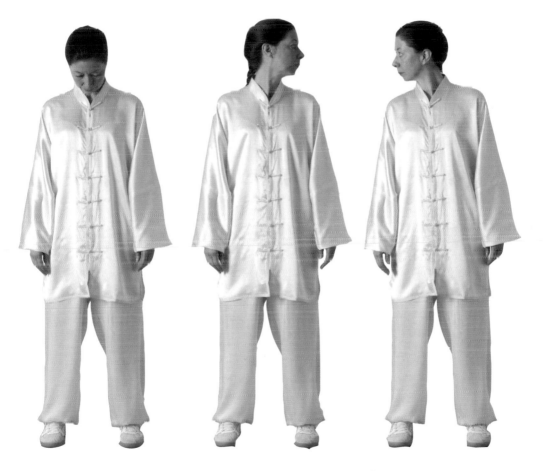

1. Standing comfortably, lower your chin onto your chest. Keeping the chin low, make slow forward rotations only.

2. Circle up to look over the left shoulder.

3. Circle down and then up to look over your right shoulder. Come back to the center and look forward. Repeat as required.

no.7 to stretch the lower back, hamstrings & calf muscles.

The muscles used in this exercise are the lower back, hamstring and calf muscles.

1. Stand with your feet slightly wider than shoulder-width apart. Bend forward from the hips, keeping your back straight.

2. Bend forward until you feel a nice stretch down the backs of the legs (but do not force anything).

Support your body weight by placing your hands on your thighs and keeping your legs naturally straight (knees not locked).

Breathe normally while holding the stretch. Do not bounce to increase the stretch. Breathe in as you slowly come up, then breathe out as you go back down into the stretch, try to increase the stretch, but always within your own range. Repeat as required.

no.8 to stretch the abdominals & oblique muscles

Stand with your feet shoulder-width apart and place your palms on your lower back for support. Stretch upward with your body until you feel all your abdominal muscles tighten. Then use that muscle group to stretch back. To increase the stretch, squeeze your elbows back until you feel a stretch in the oblique muscle group.

Repeat as required.

no.9 to stretch the calf muscles (gastronemus)

The muscles used in this group are the calf muscles and the hamstrings.

1. Stand with your feet 6–8 inches (15–20 centimeters) apart. Sink your body weight on to the left leg as you bend the knee. Make sure you knee stays in line with your toes. Place your right leg forward onto the heel, and pull the toes back until you feel a stretch in the calf muscle. Hold for a count of eight. Then place the foot flat on the floor, keeping the leg straight.

To increase this stretch, press down with your palm onto your right thigh as you pull your toes back and hold for a count of eight.

Repeat on the other side.

no.10 for knees & ankles

The muscles used in this exercise are the quadriceps, calf muscles and hamstrings.

1. Bring both feet together and bend your knees forward. (Maintain your balance.) When bending the knees forward make no more than a 90-degree angle. Come up onto the balls of your feet, activating the acupressure points in your feet.

2. Then go back onto the heels, raising the front of feet up. Repeat this eight times.

no.11 to warm up the lower limbs

This exercise prepares the lower limbs for kicking exercises.

1. Stand with your feet shoulder-width apart. Step forward with the left leg into the Forward Bow Stance, bending at the left knee. Make sure your knee does not extend further than the toes.

2. Swing your right leg forward and upward, keeping the leg straight and the toes pulled back. Maintain your body weight on your front leg, and keep your balance as you kick.

Practice this movement ten times on each side.

no.12 balance & control

The muscles in this exercise are sartorius, gluteus maximus and hamstring.

1. Stand on one leg and raise the other knee to the same level as your hip. Hold your balance and count to five. Focus your eyes on a point in front of you.

2. After a count of five, place one hand below your raised knee and the other over your foot. Pull your thigh into your body and hold to a count of five. Lower the leg to the floor and repeat the sequence on the other side.

chapter 4 **kung fu stances**

Within all martial arts there are STANCES: in Kung Fu/Wushu there are many.

The stances are the most important part of your basic training. If you do not have a strong foundation your art will be weak, just in the same way that house without a good foundation will fall down.

Each stance is a component that defines your art; whether punching, kicking, blocking or sparring, your power must be generated from your stance.

It also helps build up your upper and lower limbs, and your eye, hand and foot coordination. If your stance is strong then your art will be smooth, powerful and dynamic.

If your stance is weak then your art will be uncoordinated, loose and powerless.

Each school of Kung Fu/Wushu may use stances in different ways: within the Northern school, the stances are very low and wide, while in the Southern school they are not quite so low or wide. We look at five basic stances, which can be found in all martial arts, although the names may differ.

stances

1	Forward Bow Stance	(Gong Bu)
2	Riding Horse Stance	(Ma Bu)
3	Empty Step Stance	(Xu Bu)
4	Crouching Bow Stance	(Pu Bu)
5	Scissor Stance	(Jian Zi Gu Bu)
5a	Resting Stance	(Xie Bu)

With stances 5 & 5a the leg work is the same, but one stance is high and the other is low.

no. 1 forward bow stance (gong bu)
high stance

1. Stand with your feet 6–8 inches (15–20 cm) apart, fists on your hips.

2. Move your right foot forward (approx 2½ lengths of your own foot). Bend your front knee keeping the back leg straight. Bend the knee until the front thigh makes a 45-degree angle to the floor. Sink your weight through the front hip not the knee. Your front foot should be in line with the back heel.

Repeat sequence on the other side.

low stance

Stand with your feet 6–8 inches (15–20 cm) apart, fists on your hips. Move your left foot forward (approx 3½ lengths of your own foot). Bend your front knee, keeping your back leg straight, until the front thigh is parallel with the floor. Sink through the front hip not the knee. Your front foot should be in line with the back heel.

Repeat sequence on the other side.

forward bow stance: common mistakes

Front knee extends beyond the toe.

Thigh of bending leg not parallel to floor (low stance).

Back leg bent at knee.

Heel of back leg raised up.   Toes of back foot not pointing obliquely forward 45 degrees.

Rear hip and buttock protruding.

no. 2 riding horse stance (ma bu)
high stance

Standing with your feet together, move your left leg to the side by 2¹/₂ lengths of your foot. The toes should point forward and your fists should rest on your hips. Bend your knees until the thighs are at 45 degrees to the floor.

low stance

Standing with your feet together, move your left leg to the side by 3½ lengths of your foot. Your toes should point forward and your fists should rest on your hips. Bend your knees so that the thighs are parallel to floor.

riding horse stance: common mistakes

Toes point outward.

Back not straight.

Feet too close together.

Feet too far apart.

Knees drawn in too much.

Knees extend beyond toes.

no. 3 empty stance (xu bu)
high stance

Stand with your feet 6–8 inches (15–20 cm) apart. Move your left leg forward by two lengths of your foot, and sink your body weight into your rear leg. The thigh should be at a 45-degree angle to the floor. Hold your hands in the "on guard" position. Keep your back straight and your head erect.

low stance

Stand with your feet 6–8 inches (15–20 cm) apart. Move your left leg forward by 2½ lengths of your foot and sink your body weight into your rear leg until the thigh is parallel to floor. You should be touching the floor with just the tip of your foot. Hold your hands in the "on guard" position. Keep your back straight and head erect.

Repeat the sequence on the opposite side.

empty stance: common mistakes

Body leaning back.

Body leaning forward.

Front heel touching the ground.

Hip protruding at rear.

no. 4 crouching stance (pu bu)
high stance

Stand with your feet together and slide your left leg out by 2½ lengths of your own foot. Your thigh should be at 45 degrees to the floor.

low stance

Stand with your feet together and slide your left leg out by 3¹/₂ lengths of your own foot. Bend your right knee until your thigh is parallel to the floor. Push upward with your right arm, palm facing up, and punch forward with your left fist. Keep your back straight and the head erect. Repeat on the other side.

crouching stance: common mistakes

Heel or outer edge of squatting foot raised.

Sliding leg bent at the knee.

Leaning forward.

crouching stance: common mistakes, cont'd.

Outer edge of sliding foot raised.

Knee of squatting foot drawn in.

Toes of sliding foot not pointing inward.

no. 5 scissor stance (jian zi gu bu)

Stand with your feet shoulder-width apart. Step across your right leg with your left leg. You should be facing forward on a slight diagonal. Sit down as far as possible onto your back leg with your heel raised. Your back knee should sit in the hollow of your front knee. Keep your back straight and the head erect. Repeat on other side.

no. 5a resting stance (xie bu)

Stand with feet shoulder-width apart. Step across your right leg with your left leg. Face forward on a slight diagonal. Sit down onto your back leg so that your buttocks are touching your calf. Your lower knee should not touch the floor. Keep your back straight and the head erect. Repeat on other side.

resting stance: common mistakes

Buttocks not seated on calf of back leg.

Feet too widely separated.   Back knee not in touch with back of front knee.

chapter 5 **stance, fist & foot training**

This is to build up coordination between the upper and lower limbs, as well as coordination of eye, hand and foot. This kind of training will build speed, power and flexibility.

Chinese Kung Fu/Wushu has its own traditional training system. The exercises that follow are some of the fundamental training techniques for Northern Shaolin.

Fist and foot training are very important for coordinating the inside and outside activities. Inside activities refer to the mind, whereas outside activities refer to the bodily movements of the eye, hand and foot.

The basic requirement of the body concerns posture and stance. When standing, the body should be erect and relaxed so that it can respond to an attack from any direction. The five body parts (head, two arms and two legs) should be well balanced in order to maintain coordination between the upper and lower limbs. The hand should coordinate with the foot, the shoulder with the hip, and the elbow with the knee. These are known as the three outside coordinations—Wai San He.

Training in these fundamental techniques is the root of Northern Kung Fu. If you practice on a regular basis you will build strength, speed, agility and fluidity of movement.

riding horse stance (ma bu)

exercise 1: thrust punch (chang quan)

1. Stand with your feet in Riding Horse Stance (Ma Bu). Clench your fists and rest them on your hips with the heart of fist facing up (see page 75).

2. Punch forward with the left fist (eye of fist up), turning your shoulder and hips as you go.

3. Withdraw your left fist, rotating it so that the heart of fist is facing up. At the same time punch forward with your right fist, rotating it so that the eye of fist is facing up.

Make eight punches to the left, then eight to the right.

exercise 2: right and left bow stance (you zhou gong bu) and right and left thrust punch (you zhou chang quan)

This exercise increases the previous movement

1. Stand with your feet in Riding Horse Stance (Ma Bu). Clench the fists and rest them on your hips (heart of fist facing up).

2. As you punch forward with the left fist, turn your body to the right, turning your right foot out and sliding your left foot back to a 45-degree angle (so you move into right Bow Stance— Gong Bu) as you thrust punch (eye of fist up). Your eyes should focus on the punching hand.

3. As you withdraw your left fist, rotate so that the heart of fist is facing up. At the same time turn your body back into Riding Horse Stance (Ma Bu), drawing the right foot back.

important points

1	You can practice this in either high or low stance
2	You are turning your body to a 90-degree angle, keep your back straight and head erect
3	Eyes focused on punching hand
4	Make sure your bow stance is strong and beware of knee extending beyond the toe

4. Return to the Riding Horse Stance (Ma Bu).

5. Repeat this movement on the opposite side.

Practice this very slowly at first until you get the coordination. Practice eight punches on each side.

exercise 3: right and left resting stance (you zhou xir bu) and right and left thrust punch (you zhou chang quan)

1. Stand in the Riding Horse Stance (Ma Bu).

2. Punch with your right fist as you step back with your left leg behind the right leg.

3. Squat down into the Resting Stance (Xie Bu), with your buttocks resting on your calf.

4. Reverse the movement back to the Riding Horse Stance (Ma Bu).

Then repeat the sequence on other side.

5. Punch with your left fist, as you begin to step back, with the right leg behind the left leg.

important points

1	Coordinate your punching and leg work
2	When in Resting Stance, keep your back straight and head erect
3	Buttocks should touch the back of your calf
4	Eyes should focus on the punching fist

6. Squat down into the Resting Stance (Xie Bu), with your buttocks resting on your calf.

7. Reverse the movement to return to the Riding Horse Stance (Ma Bu).

Make eight punches on each side.

front snap kick (che chuai)

exercise 4

1. Stand with your feet shoulder-width apart. This is the Spring Leg Kick (Tan Tui).

2. Sink your body weight onto the left leg, so that the right leg is empty with just the toe touching the floor (Empty Step—Xu Bu). Keep your fists on your hips.

3. Raise your right knee up as high as you can.

4. Kick forward with the right foot, pointing the toes forward, and sink more of your body weight onto the left leg. Keep good balance and transfer the power into your right kick.

5. Bring the lower part of your right leg back down so that the knee is raised as high as it will go.

6. Then lower the right foot to the floor and center your balance, standing back with both feet shoulder-width apart.

Repeat on the other side, with eight each time.

points to remember

1	When kicking, hold your balance
2	Do not lean back as you kick
3	Do not kick higher than waist level
4	Practice slowly to build up the power in your legs
5	Only sink as low as is comfortable for you in Empty Stance
6	Check that you feel the muscles in the thigh working
7	If you feel discomfort in the knee joint check your stance

If you want to change the working muscle groups in your leg while kicking, all you have to do is pull the toes back and kick with the heel.

There is a much stronger stretch in the calf muscle – a kick called Heel Kick – Deng Tui (see page 87).

exercise 5: combining thrust punches (chang quan)

The next training session is to help with the coordination of the hands and feet.

1. Stand with your feet 6–8 inches (15–20 cm) apart and step forward into the left Bow Stance. Place your left fist on your left hip. Bring your right fist forward into a thrust punch at shoulder level.

2. Sink your body weight on to your left leg, then kick with the right foot to waist height, and with toes pointing forward. At the same time, punch forward with your left fist (eye of fist up). Both foot and fist should arrive at the same time.

3. Reverse the movement, returning to your starting position of left Bow Stance, right fist forward.

Repeat on the opposite side.

2. Now punch with your right fist, while kicking with your left foot, toes pointing forward.

1. Stand in the right Bow Stance, with your left fist forward.

3. Reverse the movement, returning to the right Bow Stance with left fist forward.

Practice the movement ten times on each side.

points to remember

1	**Keep body at the same height as you kick and punch**
2	**Keep back straight as you kick (don't dip)**
3	**Keep head erect as you punch**
4	**Coordinate your kick and punch**
5	**Eyes should focus on your kick and punch**

You can also use the heel kick during practice (see below). All punching movements can be changed to palm strikes, so you can train yourself to use the heel of the hand instead.

It is important that while you are training in these techniques, you should always train within your own capability. Start all exercises slowly then, as your coordination improves, you will find that your speed and power develop too.

The old Masters would train on one technique for many months to perfect it, and for many years to perfect the techniques as a whole.

hand & foot techniques
chapter 6 – northern style

Within the Northern and Southern styles the striking and kicking techniques vary considerably. These techniques are for reference, so you can see some of the movement in Northern Kung Fu/Wushu.

But if you want to practice these techniques they will help to coordinate your upper and lower limbs and your eye, hand and foot. Your shoulders will coordinate with your hips, your elbows with your knees and your hands with your feet.

The Northern schools have a striking range that is normally a much longer range. The striking is based on:

fist (quan)

Tightly clench your fist with the knuckles even. Place your thumb across the mid section of the index finger and the middle finger.

eye of fist

heart of fist

face of fist

heel of fist

palm (zhang)

Hold your fingers together and straight, keeping the palm flat. Tuck your thumb into the side of your palm.

hook (gou)

Flex your hand at the wrist with all four fingers touching your thumb.

fist techniques (quan fa)

thrust punch (chong quan)

As you move forward into the Bow Stance (You Gong Bu), rotate your fist forward in line with your shoulders. The face of fist knuckles should be even and the eye of fist up. Power is applied to the face of fist.

Practice movement eight times on each side.

straight arm chop (pi quan)

Circle your right fist over the top of your head, finishing in line with your shoulder. Power is applied to the bottom of the fist. Circle your left palm above your head with the palm facing upward. Bring your feet together (Bing Bu).

Practice the movement eight times on each side.

hammer strike (za quan)

1. Raise your right fist above your head and raise the knee on the same side up to hip height.

2. Smash the back of your fist downward into the other palm with power applied to the back of the fist. At the same time stamp your foot on the ground.

Practice the movement eight times on each side.

uppercut (liao quan)

From the Riding Horse Stance (Ma Bu), push your left forearm out in front of you, parallel to your chest. Sweep your left forearm down to knee level and then up in line with your left shoulder. Turn your body into the left Bow Stance (Zhou Gong Bu) and circle the right fist upward to shoulder level (eye of fist up). Power is applied to the eye of fist.

Practice the movement
eight times on each side.

palm techniques (zhang fa)

push palm (tui zhang)

Step forward into the left Bow Stance (Zhou Gong Bu), with your left palm striking forward, from your hip to level with your shoulder. keep your fingers together and your thumb tucked into the side of your palm.

Practice the movement eight times on each side.

palm chop (qie zhang)

Sit down into a right Crouch Stance (You Pu Bu) and bring your right fist into the hip of the bent thigh. Outstretch the left arm in line with the left leg with the palm edge facing outward. Power is applied to the outer edge of the palm.

Practice the movement eight times on each side.

elbow parry (ger zhou)

In the Riding Horse Stance (Ma Bu) bring your forearm in front of your body, fist level with chest and elbow slightly bent. Power is applied to forearm.

Practice the movement eight times on each side.

hook elbow (pan zhou)

In the forward right Bow Stance (You Gong Bu) and from an outstretched arm, bend your elbow in front of your body at a 90-degree angle. Power is applied to front part of forearm.

Practice the movement eight times on each side.

elbowing (ding zhou)

Step forward into the left Bow Stance (Zhou Gong Bu), thrust your elbow forward with the tip of the elbow pointing forward. The opposite palm should push against the fist. Power is applied to the elbow.

Practice the movement eight times on each side.

leg techniques(tui fa)

Within the Northern system, there are many kicking techniques, hence the expression "Northern Leg." These techniques will increase your stamina and flexibility and will strengthen your legs. I will name just a few.

front kick

Stand with your feet 6–8 inches (15–20 cm) apart with your fists on your hips, heart of fist up. Raise the right knee as high as it will go and kick forward with toes pointing forward. To build up balance and strength, focus the power through the toes. Hold for a slow count of five and repeat on the other side.

Practice the movement eight times on each side.

front snap heel-kick (deng tui)

Stand with your feet 6–8 inches (15–20 cm) apart with your fists on your hips, heart of fist up. Raise the right knee as high as it will go and kick forward, pulling the toes back. The power is applied through the heel of the foot. Repeat on the opposite side.

Practice the movement eight times on each side.

spring leg kick (tan tui)

Stand with your feet shoulder-width apart. Sinking your body weight into your rear leg, bring the other leg up so that your thigh is level with your hip. Snap the leg out in front of you with your toes pointing forward. Power is applied to the toes.

Practice the movement eight times on each side.

front kick (zheng ti tui)

Swing your right leg up directly in front of your body, keeping the leg straight. Keep your supporting leg stable to control your balance. Power is applied to the heel. Keep your arms level with your shoulders, palms facing out.

Practice the movement eight times on each side.

oblique kick (xie ti tui)

Swing your right leg diagonally across your body, keeping the leg and your back straight. Make sure that your supporting leg is stable. Power is applied to the heel. Keep your arms level with your shoulders, palms facing out.

Practice the movement eight times on each side.

side kick (che ti tui)

Swing your right leg out to the side of your body, keeping the leg straight. Raise your right arm above the head, palm facing up. Bend your left arm at the elbow in front of your chest, left palm facing left. Keep your supporting leg stable to control your balance. Power is applied to the heel.

Practice the movement eight times on each side.

inside crescent kick (li he tui)

Standing with your arms outstretched, palms facing forward, swing your left leg in an inward arc in front of your body. Keeping the leg straight, touch the sole of the left foot to the palm of the right hand. Keep your back and supporting leg straight. Power is applied to the sole of your foot.

Practice the movement
eight times on each side.

outside crescent kick (way bai tui)

Standing with your arms outstretched, palms facing forward, swing your right leg in an outward arc in front of your body. Keeping the leg straight, touch the heel of the right foot to the palm of the right hand. Keep your back and supporting leg straight. Power is applied to the sole of your foot

Practice the movement eight times on each side.

hand & foot techniques
chapter 7 – southern style

Southern style hand techniques: there are many more hand and arm (bridge) techniques than in the Northern style, hence the expression "Southern Fist." Southern styles are famous for their dynamic (bridge) training techniques, as will be described.

fist (quan)

Hold your fist lightly clenched with the knuckles even. Place your thumb across the mid section on the index finger and the middle finger.

palm (zhang)

Hold your fingers together and straight, keeping the palm flat. Tuck your thumb into the side of your palm.

eye of fist

heart of fist

face of fist

heel of fist

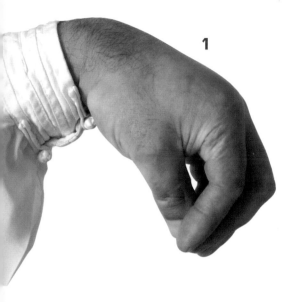

1

1. hook (gou)

Flex your hand at the wrist with all four fingers touching your thumb.

tiger paw (hu zhao)

Spread your fingers and hook the second and third joints of the fingers, and the second joint of the thumb, so that the palm is exposed. The hand should be flexed back slightly.

eagle claw (ying zhao)

Open the hand out fully, then hook the fingers at the first knuckle. Draw the thumb back to the edge of the palm. Keep the palm exposed and flex the wrist back slightly.

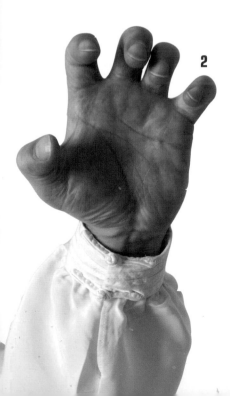

2

3

single finger (dang zhi)

Flex the wrist back, with the index finger pointing upward. Curl the other three fingers in and tuck the thumb into the side of the palm. This is to strengthen the forearm (bridge).

4

crane's bill (he zui shou)

Connect the tips of the four fingers and the thumb without flexing the wrist.

5

punching techniques (quan fa)

thrust punch (chong quan)

Step forward into the left Bow Stance (Zhou Gong Bu) with your right fist at waist level. Punch forward with the right arm, rotating the eye of fist upward, and keeping the knuckles on the face of fist even. Raise the left palm to face the right forearm.

Practice the movement eight times on each side.

tossing chop (pao quan)

Step forward into right left Bow Stance (Zhou Gong Bu). Punch up with the left fist as you punch out with the right. Coordinate both arm movements. Power is focused to eye of fist.

Practice the movement eight times on each side.

covering strike (gai quan)

From the Riding Horse Stance (Ma Bu) turn into the left Bow Stance (Zhou Gong Bu). Circle the right arm up over your head with the fist striking downward. Power is focused to the heart of fist.

Practice the movement eight times on each side.

flail fist (bian quan)

Standing in Empty Step (Xu Bu), move your arms across your body at shoulder height. Clench the right fist and hold the left palm by the right shoulder. Power is applied to the back of fist.

Practice the movement eight times on each side.

thrust fist (zhuang quan)

Step into the right Bow Stance (Zhou Gong Bu).
With a follow-up step, punch out in front of you
with your right arm, heart of fist up. Place your left
palm on your right forearm. Power is applied to
the face of fist.

Practice the movement eight times on each side.

palm techniques (zhang fa)

tilt palm (tiao zhang)

In Riding Horse Stance (Ma Bu), with arms outstretched, and palms at shoulder level, curve the palms in an outward movement. The power is from down to up. Power is applied to fingers.

Practice the movement eight times

palm push (tui zhang)

Step forward into the left Bow Stance (Zhou Gong Bu) with follow-up step. Push the palms forward, keeping your elbows and shoulders level and all four fingers together. Power is applied to center of the palms.

Practice the movement eight times on each side.

palm hack (pi zhang)

Stand in right Empty Step (You Xu Bu), with your left arm outstretched, palm facing inward. Keeping the fingers together, chop the palm downward. Power is applied to the outer edge of palm.

Practice the movement eight times on each side.

palm thrust (biao zhuang)

Stand in Riding Horse Stance (Ma Bu) with your palms on your hips. Thrust forward with both hands, fingers together and pointing forward. Power is applied to fingertips.

Practice eight times.

elbow strikes (zhou ta)

upward elbow strike (dan zhou)

Stand in Riding Horse Stance (Ma Bu) with your fists resting on your hips. Draw both elbows upward in a quick forceful movement. Originate the power from your waist. Power is applied to the elbows.

Practice the movement eight times.

elbow press (ya yhou)

This is the single Butterfly Stance (Dan Die Bu). Bend your arm across the front of your body, with the forearm to the front. Press down with the elbow. Power is applied to elbow.

Practice the movement eight times on each side.

southern bridge techniques (qiao fa)

The specialist technique of Southern Fist is the training of the forearm in order to create powerful bridge (arm) movements.

intercept bridge (jie qiao)

Step forward into the left Bow Stance (Zhou Gong Bu) with your right arm in a blocking movement to the side of your body. Rotate the forearm. Power is applied to the forearm.

Practice the movement eight times on each side.

chop bridge (pi qiao)

In Riding Horse Stance (Ma Bu), bring your right arm across your body. From left to right, make a sideways strike at shoulder level. The power is applied to the back of the forearm.

Practice the movement eight times on each side.

threading bridge (chuan qiao)

In Scissor Stance (Jian Zi Gu Bu), step forward with one arm passing under the other. Thread the passing arm forward as you make the movement. Power is applied to the fingers.

Practice the movement eight times on each side.

sinking bridge (cheng qiao)

Stand in Empty Step (Xu Bu) with elbows bent, and hands by your shoulders. Flex the wrists downward with the index fingers pointing up. Sink from up to down. This movement strengthens the forearms. Power is applied to the forearms.

Practice the movement eight times.

roll bridge (gueng qiao)

Stand in the forward Bow Stance (Gong Bu). Stretch the left arm out in front of you while pulling the right arm back. Power is applied to front fist and back forearm.

Practice the movement eight times on both sides.

kicking techniques (tui fa)

front kick (teng kong fei jiao)

1. Take two steps forward, using the left leg as a springboard.

2. Jump up and bring the right leg up.

3. Snap the kick forward. The power is applied to the right toes.

nail kick (hung ding tui)

Step forward with your right leg, placing your weight onto the left leg. Kick the right leg forward across your body with the foot at an angle. The power is applied to the toes.

Practice the movement eight times on each side.

The internal styles have many striking techniques using the fist, palm and the hook. Here is a brief explanation of what makes each system unique.

Taijiquan is based on the eight energies of the hand, arm and shoulder, which are Peng, Lui, Ji An, Chai, Lia, Jou and Kou. The five stepping principles are center, forward, backward, left and right. Taijiquan is a soft, light and slow exercise which features continuous circular and fluent hand and foot movements.

Baghua Zhang specializes in the different eight palm techniques and features special footwork and turning of the body. It uses changing palm techniques of pushing, holding, carrying, leading, thrusting, cutting and blocking. The practitioner walks a circle and then crisscrosses in all directions. It features swift body movements, flexible footwork and constant changes of direction.

Xingyiquan has very special fist movements known as spiral fist (Luosi). Xingyiquan always starts with a stance, in which the body weight is mostly on the back leg (San Ti Shi). The five basic fist movements are: splitting fist, crushing fist, drilling fist, cannon fist and crossing fist.

These techniques will be explained in more detail within the Xingyiquan Form, later in this book.

a brief history of tan tui

(northern spring leg,shaolin kung fu)

The first style of Kung Fu/Wushu I would like to introduce to you is Tan Tui, Northern Spring Leg Shaolin. This is an "external" (hard) style.

The original Tan Tui is called Longtantui (Longtan foot play). According to legend Tan Tui came from the Longtan Monastery in the Shandong Province, hence the name of the style. It is now more commonly known as Tan Tui.

Tan Tui has twelve routines, of which this book looks at the first. The twelve routines encompass the basics of Northern Shaolin and many northern schools use Tan Tui as a fundamental part of their teaching syllabus. Tan Tui is a style in its own right and has many training practices within its art.

In 1910 the Jingwu Sports Society incorporated Tan Tui into its training schedule. It has ten differing schools of martial arts and uses them as basic training within their teaching of Kung Fu/Wushu systems.

In China, Tan Tui is one of the exercises included on the national curriculm. It has been highlighted as a very good discipline in helping to build personal development and for strengthening the body.

The specialist technique of Tan Tui is the snapping of the kicking foot, and it is because of this that the discipline has the name Spring Leg Kung Fu.

The importance of practicing Tan Tui skills is to make each movement well coordinated with a smooth transition from one stance to another. The form is practiced on both sides of the body.

The stances are very low, which helps to build strength and flexibility in the legs. The punching and blocking in Tan Tui is performed with speed, power and vigor.

There is an old Chinese saying "if your attacker is strong, then you must be stronger in counterattack." The movements of Tan Tui are very simple, but with the correct training it can be a devastating art for self-defense.

tan tui – 1st section

1st section prepare posture (ye bei)

1. Stand with your feet together, back straight and arms down by your side. Hold your head erect.

2. Bring your fists up to your hips.

1st section posture 1 – feet together, right thrust punch (bing bu you chong quan)

1. Keeping your feet together, bend your right elbow and bring the fist up in front of your right shoulder.

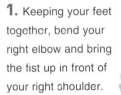

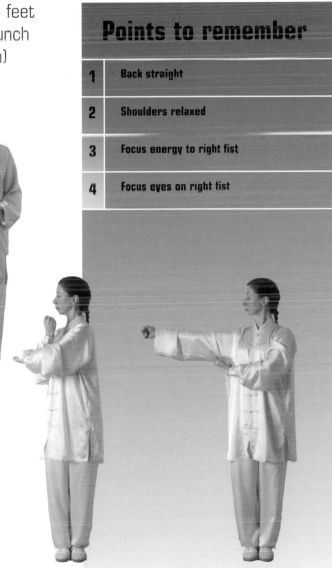

Points to remember

1	Back straight
2	Shoulders relaxed
3	Focus energy to right fist
4	Focus eyes on right fist

2. Raise your left palm above your head.

3. Turn your upper body to the right and lower your left arm, palm facing out.

4. Punch your right fist out to the right side at shoulder level. Focus your eyes on the right fist (eye of fist up).

1st section posture 2 – riding horse stance & elbow parry (mabu ger zhou)

Continuing from the last movement, open your left leg and sit down into the Riding Horse Stance. Bring your left arm across the body and press down with the left forearm. Form a fist with the left hand, heart of fist pointing up. Keep your right fist out to the right, level with your shoulder. Eyes should focus forward toward your left fist.

Points to remember

1	**Riding Horse Stance (toes point forward, knees in line with toes)**
2	**Right fist should be level with shoulder**
3	**Keep back straight**
4	**Focus energy to left forearm**

1st section posture 3 – left forward bow stance thrust punch (zhou gong bu chong quan)

Points to remember

1	Forward bow stance, make sure knee and toes are in alignment
2	Knee does not extend beyond the toe
3	Back leg straight, toe at a 45-degree angle
4	Relax shoulders
5	Focus energy to left fist

1. Continuing from the last movement draw your left fist into the hip.

2. Turn your body to the left, twisting the left foot. Bend your left knee into a left forward Bow Stance, adjusting the back heel to a 45-degree angle and thrust punch with your left fist, eye of fist up. Keep both arms in line with your shoulders and both fists clenched. Focus on the left fist.

1st section posture 4 – horse riding stance & elbow strike (mabu ding zhou)

1. Continuing from the last movement, turn your body back to the right, facing forward.

2. Adjust the positions of your feet, so that both point forward. Bend your knees to sit down into the Riding Horse Stance.

Points to remember

1	Riding Horse Stance, toes point forward
2	Knees in line with toes
3	Keep back straight and head erect
4	Focus energy to elbow

3. Bend your left arm in front of and parallel to your chest, elbow pointing to the left, heart of fist down. Focus eyes toward the left elbow.

1st section posture 5 – left forward bow stance, uppercut with right fist (zhou gong bu liao quan)

1. Continuing from the last movement, turn your body to the left into a left forward Bow Stance. Sweep the left fist down and out at knee level and up in line with your left shoulder, eye of fist up.

2. Sweep the right fist down in a forward movement.

3. Raise arm in front of body, chin level and eye of fist up. Focus eyes on right fist.

1st section posture 6 – circle right fist downward (you za quan)

1. Continuing from the last movement, circle your right fist inward.

Points to remember	
1	**Focus energy to back of right fist**
2	**Shoulders relaxed**
3	**Focus energy to right fist**
4	**Eyes focused on right fist**

2. and downward, using back of fist.

3. Keep your right fist level with the hip and left fist level with the left shoulder.

1st section posture 7 – forward right snap kick (you tan tui)

This completes the first section of the routine. The next section uses the same moves but on the other side of the body. Make sure you are competent with the first section before you move on to the next section: it is better to learn a few movements correctly than many movements incorrectly.

Points to remember

1	Hold your balance when you kick
2	Back straight, head erect
3	Focus energy to right toe

1. Continuing from the last movement, keep your fists in same position and draw the right knee forward and up.

2. Snap the right leg forward to groin height with toes pointing forward.

tan tui – 2nd section

2nd section posture 1 – riding horse stance elbow parry (mabu ger zhou)

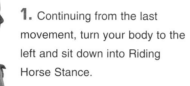

1. Continuing from the last movement, turn your body to the left and sit down into Riding Horse Stance.

Points to remember

1	**Riding Horse Stance, toes point forward**
2	**Knees in line with toes**
3	**Keep back straight and head erect**
4	**Focus energy to right forearm**

2. Adjust your feet so that toes point forward.

3. Bring the right fist in front of your body, forearm pressing down, heart of fist pointing up (level with chest). Keep the left fist level with your left shoulder. Eyes focus forward toward the right fist.

2nd section posture 2 – right forward bow stance, right thrust punch (you gong bu chong quan)

1. Continuing from the last movement, draw your right fist into the hip.

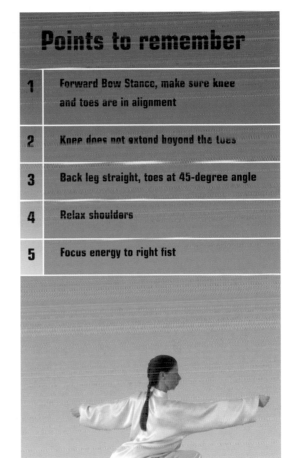

2. Turn your body to the right, turning the right foot out to the right.

3. Bend your front knee into a right forward Bow Stance, adjust the back heel to a 45-degree angle and thrust punch with your right fist, eye of fist up. Keep both arms in line with your shoulders and keep your fists clenched. Eyes focus toward the right fist.

2nd section posture 3 – horse riding stance elbow strike (ma bu ding zhou)

Points to remember

1	**Riding Horse Stance, toes point forward**
2	**Knees in line with toes**
3	**Keep back straight and head erect**
4	**Focus energy to the elbow**

1. Continuing from the last movement, turn your body to the left, hook the right foot around and adjust the left foot so both feet point forward. Bend your knees and sit down into Riding Horse Stance. Bend your right arm parallel to and in front of your chest.

2. Point your elbow to the right, heart of fist down. Keep the left fist parallel with your left shoulder. Eyes focus toward the right elbow.

2nd section posture 4 – right forward bow stance (you gong bu (liao quan)

Points to remember

1	Right arm is a blocking movement
2	Posture alignment
3	Right uppercut is a counterattack
4	Energy focus on the left fist

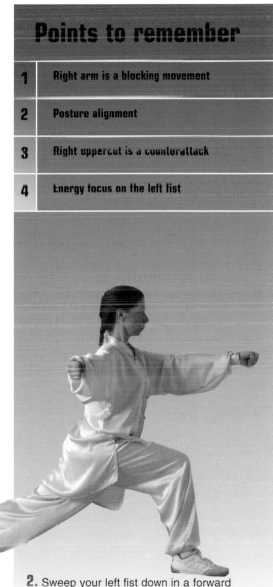

1. Continuing from the last movement, turn your body to the right Into a right forward Bow Stance. Sweep your right fist down and across at knee level and up in line with your right shoulder, eye of fist up.

2. Sweep your left fist down in a forward movement to uppercut in front of your body at chin level, eye of fist up. Eyes focus to the left fist.

2nd section posture 5 - circle left fist downward (zhou za quan)

1. Continuing from the last movement, circle your left fist inward.

2. Then circle the left fist downward.

Points to remember

1	Focus energy to back of fist

3. Your left fist should be level with your hip while the right fist stays level with the right shoulder. Focus eyes on the back of your fist.

2nd section posture 6 – left forward snap kick (zhou tan tui)

This finishes the second section of the routine. The third section is a repeat of the first section.

Practice both sections until you have committed each movement to memory.

Points to remember

1	**Hold your balance when you kick**
2	**Keep back straight and head erect**
3	**Focus your energy to the left toes**

1. Continuing from the last movement, and keeping your fists in the same position, draw the left knee forward and up.

2. Snap the left leg forward, toes pointing forward at groin height.

3rd section

3rd section posture 1 – riding horse stance & elbow parry (mabu ger zhou)

1. Continuing from the last movement, step down.

Points to remember

1	Riding Horse stance (toes point forward, knees in line with toes)
2	Right fist should be level with shoulder
3	Keep back straight
4	Focus energy to the left forearm

2. Turn your body to the right.

3. Sit down into a Riding Horse Stance. Bring your left arm across the body and press down with your forearm, heart of fist pointing up. Keep the right fist out to right side, level with your shoulder. Eyes focus forward toward the left fist.

3rd section posture 2 – left forward bow stance thrust punch (zhou gong bu chong quan)

1. Continuing from the last movement draw your left fist into the hip.

2. Turn your body to the left and turn the left foot out to the left. Bend your front knee into a left forward Bow Stance, adjusting the back heel to a 45-degree angle and thrust. Punch with the left fist, eye of fist up. Keep both arms in line with shoulders with fists clenched.

3rd section posture 3 – horse riding stance & elbow strike (mabu ding zhou)

1. Continuing from the last movement, turn your body to the right (front).

Points to remember

1	**Riding Horse Stance (toes point forward, knees in line with toes)**
2	**Right fist should be level with shoulder**
3	**Keep back straight**
4	**Focus energy to left elbow**

2. Hook your left foot around and adjust the right foot, so that both feet point forward. Bend your knees and sit down into Riding Horse Stance.

3. Bend the left arm parallel to and in front of your chest, elbow pointing to the left, heart of fist down. Keep the right fist parallel with your shoulder. Eyes focus toward the left elbow.

3rd section posture 4 – left forward bow stance, uppercut with right fist (zhou gong bu liao quan)

1. Continuing from the last movement, turn your body to the left into a left forward Bow Stance.

2. Sweep your left fist down and across at knee level and up in line with your left shoulder, eye of fist up.

3. Sweep the right fist down in a forward movement to uppercut to the front of your body at chin level, eye of fist up. Eyes focus to the right fist.

3rd section posture 5 – circle right fist downward (you za quan)

1. Continuing from the last movement circle your right fist inward.

Points to remember

1	**Focus energy to back of fist**

3. Keep the right fist level with hip and the left fist level with the left shoulder.

2. Then circle it downward, using the back of your fist.

3rd section posture 6 – forward right snap kick (you tan tui)

Points to remember

1	Hold your balance when you kick
2	Keep back straight and head erect
3	Focus your energy to the right toe

1. Continuing from the last movement, keep your fists in same position and draw the right knee forward and up.

2. Snap the leg forward, toe pointing forward, to groin height.

3rd section posture 7 – riding horse stance elbow parry (mabu ger zhou)

1. Continuing from the last movement, turn your body to the left and sit down into Riding Horse Stance.

Points to remember

1	**Riding Horse stance, toes point forward**
2	**Knees in line with toes**
3	**Keep back straight and head erect**
4	**Focus energy to the right forearm**

2. Adjust your feet so that toes point forward.

3. Bring the right fist in front of your body, forearm pressing down, heart of fist pointing up (level with chest). Keep the left fist level with your left shoulder. Eyes focus forward toward the right fist.

3rd section posture 8 – right forward bow stance & thrust punch (you gong bu chong quan)

2. Turn your right foot out into a right forward Bow Stance

1. Turn your body to the right.

3. Thrust your right fist out at shoulder height, eye of fist up. Keep the left fist level with your left shoulder.

closing movement (shou shi)

1. With both fists in line with shoulders, circle your left fist over your head, changing the fist to an open hand, palm down.

2. At the same time bring your right fist into your hip.

3. Bring your left foot in level with the right and thrust punch with the right fist at shoulder height, left palm facing outward under your arm.

4. Eyes focus to your right fist.

Points to remember

1	**You will be facing in the opposite direction (as first section posture 1).**

Practice these three sections again until you have committed the movements to memory. Train diligently.

You have now completed the first form of the Northern Spring Leg Kung Fu/Wushu Tan Tui.

Grasping the essence of Tan Tui will take much practice. Concentrate on building up your upper and lower limb coordination and your eye, hand and foot coordination to achieve the power of Tan Tui.

These are the basic principles of Tan Tui.

chapter 9 tan tui for self-protection

The majority of students practice martial arts for health and fitness reasons and this, therefore, is the focus of regular club training. Training at competition level is far more intensive than regular club training, while the focus for self-defense training is different yet again.

The postures for self-defense are not as low as those for other purposes. Low stances are ideal for conditioning the body, for building strength, suppleness and agility. There is a Chinese saying: "If you are strong in a low posture, when you stand normally you are much stronger."

The self-defense techniques that follow are a sequence of defensive maneuvers that can be used to foil various attacks. For example: a stranglehold, a punch to the face, a grab to the front of the body, a kick to the body, and grabbing the wrist.

These self-defense movements should give you an idea on how the form can work. Every teacher will use the postures/techniques in a different way, depending on the training he or she has done. It is still important to train the body on both sides so that you can react to any situation that may arise, from any angle.

Remember, however, that best form of self defense is not to be there in the first place.

posture 1
feet together, thrust punch (bing bu chong quan)

Defense from an attacker who is trying to strangle you.

1. Being strangled.

2. Turn your body so that you are side-on to your attacker. This movement protects the front of your body. Swing the outside arm behind you and up.

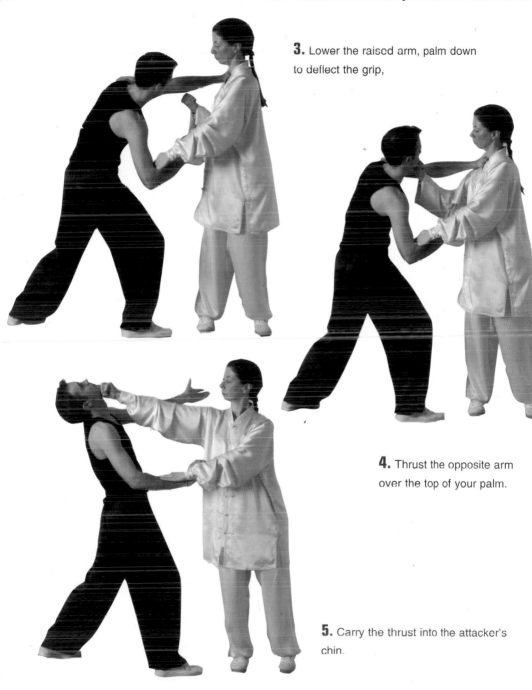

3. Lower the raised arm, palm down to deflect the grip,

4. Thrust the opposite arm over the top of your palm.

5. Carry the thrust into the attacker's chin.

postures 2 & 3
posture 2 riding horse stance (ma bu ger zhou) linking to
posture 3 forward bow stance & thrust punch (gong bu chong quan)

Defense from an attacker punching forward into your face.

1. Turn your body and step into the Riding Horse Stance.

2. At the same, and using the arm nearest your attacker, strike down with your forearm onto his or her elbow. This action is not a block but a strike.

3. Turn your body into a forward Bow Stance and thrust punch into your attacker's ribs.

posture 4
riding horse stance & elbow strike (ma bu ding zhou)

Defense from an attacker with a grab to the front of your body.

1. Step sideways into a Riding Horse Stance and block the grab with your forearm.

2. Grip your attacker's wrist and pull forward to make him lose balance.

3. Turn your body into a Bow Stance and strike with your elbow into your attacker's ribs.

posture 5
forward bow stance, uppercut with fist (gong bu liao quan)

Defense from an attacker who is kicking forward toward your body.

1. In a Riding Horse Stance, deflect the kick by sweeping the arm nearest your attacker downward.

2. Sweep the arm up again so that your arm is under your attacker's leg.

3. Step forward into the Bow Stance and sweep your other fist up, into your attacker's groin.

postures 6 & 7
posture 6 circle fist downward (za quan),
posture 7 forward snap kick (tan tui)

Defense from an attacker gripping your wrist.

1. As your attacker grips your wrist, move into a Riding Horse Stance.

2. Circle the grasped fist inward.

3. Thrust the grasped wrist down to break your attacker's grip.

4. Step forward into the Bow Stance and snap kick into your attacker's groin with your opposite leg.

5. into your attackers groin.

xingyiquan
chapter 10 (mind & will kung fu)

Xingyiquan is one of the "internal" martial arts from China, with a history of over 300 years. It is based on the Chinese five-element theory, which incorporates the five basic fists.

a brief history

With origins dating back to the Ming (1368–1644) and Qing (1644–1911) dynasties, Xingyiquan has also been known as "six harmonies boxing" (Liu He Quan).

There are there different schools of Xingyiquan: the Shanxi Province, the Henan Province and the Hebei Province. However, it must also be stressed that there are many variations within these forms.

According to historical records the creators of Xingyiquan are mostly credited as being General Ye Fei (Song Dynasty, 11th century) and Long Feng (Qing Dynasty, 17th century). At this time the spear was known as the king of weapons and Xingyiquan was developed to make the twisting, turning and speed of the fist emulate the spear.

From early records it is clearly stated that Xingyiquan placed great emphasis on health as well as fighting. The main characteristic of Xingyiquan is the San Ti Shi Posture, which is a 60–40 weight distribution, 60 percent on the back leg and 40 percent on the front leg.

The basic requirements of Xingyiquan

Xingyiquan is characterized by simple and steady movements and very powerful and direct compact routines. The system was made popular during the late 19th century by a very famous master called Sun Lu Tang who became a legend in China for his fighting skills and was known as the modern-day Monkey King. The basic requirements of the discipline are: the Body of the Dragon, the Shoulders of the Bear, the Leg of the Chicken, the Hands of an Eagle, the Arms of a Tiger and the Voice of Thunder.

Xingyiquan is based on the Chinese five-element theory and twelve animals, which incorporates the five basic fists:

Splitting Fist	Pin Quan – Metal
Crushing Fist	Beng Quan – Wood
Drilling Fist	Zuan Quan – Water
Cannon Fist	Pao Quan – Fire
Crossing Fist	Heng Quan – Earth

THE 12 ANIMALS ARE:	
Dragon, Long Xing	**Tiger, Huxing**
Monkey, Hou Xing	**Crocodile, Tuo Xing**
Horse, Ma Xing	**Cockerel, Ji Xing**
Sparrow Hawk, Yao Xing	**Swallow, Yan Xing**
Snake, Shr Xing	**Rhea, Tai Xing**
Eagle, Ying Xing	**Bear, Xiong Xing**

five-element theory

By observing and contemplating the workings of the Universe, the Ancient Chinese devised a theory to explain the balance of complimentary and antagonistic units of which it is composed. The characteristics and relationships of these dynamic units are explained in the five-elements theory.

In this theory, the Life Force in all of its myriad manifestations comes into and goes out of its existence through the interplay of the five elements:

Fire

Earth

Metal

Water

Wood

There are two cycles that illustrate the interaction between these elements. In the cycle of generation, each element generates or produces the succeeding element: Wood produces Fire, Fire produces Earth, Earth produces Metal, Metal produces Water and Water produces Wood.

In the cycle of destruction, each element destroys or absorbs the succeeding element: Fire destroys Metal, Metal destroys Wood, Wood destroys Earth, Earth absorbs Water, and Water destroys Fire.

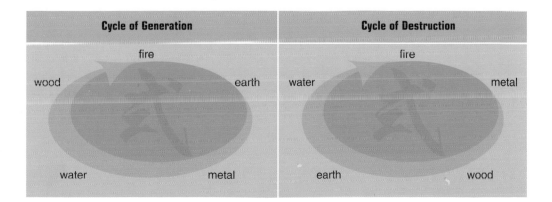

Cycle of Generation	**Cycle of Destruction**
fire	fire
wood earth	water metal
water metal	earth wood

five-element theory

Xingyi	Pi	Beng	Zuan	Pao	Heng
Movement	Split Fist	Crushing Fist	Drilling Fist	Cannon Fist	Crossing Fist
Element	METAL	WOOD	WATER	FIRE	EARTH
Yin Organ	Lung 3 AM–5 AM	Liver 1 AM–3 AM	Kidney 5 PM–7 PM	Heart 11 AM–1 PM	Spleen 9 AM–11 AM
Direction	West	East	North	South	Center
Season	Autumn	Spring	Winter	Summer	Long Summer
Colour	White	Green	Black	Red	Yellow
Taste	Pungent	Sour	Salty	Bitter	Sweet
Sensory Organ	Nose	Eye	Ear	Tongue	Mouth

Xingyi	Pi	Beng	Zuan	Pao	Heng
Emotion	Grief	Anger	Fear	Happiness	Sympathy
Sound	Weeping	Shouting	Groaning	Laughter	Singing
Condition	Dry	Windy	Cold	Heat	Damp
Smell	Rotten	Rancid	Putrid	Scorched	Fragrant
Yin Organ Stores	Qi	Blood	Jing	Blood Vessel	Nutrient
Yang Organ	Large Intestine 5 AM–7 AM	Gall Bladder 11 PM–1 AM	Urinary Bladder 3 PM–5 PM	Small Intestine 1 PM–3 PM	Stomach 7 AM–9 AM
Body Parts	Skin/Hair	Tendons	Bones & Bone Marrow	Blood Vessels	Flesh

five fists/elements of xingyiquan kung fu (wu xing quan)

The five elements of metal, wood, water, fire and earth link to the basic five fists of Xingyiquan Kung Fu:

1 Splitting/Chopping Fist	Pi Quan
2 Crushing Fist	Beng Quan
3 Drilling Fist	Zuan Quan
4 Cannon Fist	Pao Quan
5 Swing/Crossing Fist	Heng Quan

This is a sequence of forms that uses a series of fist movements to help stimulate your internal organs. Xingyiquan postures/stances are considerably different to what you have practiced in the Northern Spring Leg. They are not quite as low, but are still very dynamic.

The main posture of Xingyiquan is the most fundamental part of the training; the posture is called San Ti Shi and is known as Heaven, Earth and Man or the Three Bodies Posture.

Within the different schools of Xingyiquan the guidelines for the San Ti Shi Posture are the same, and there is a saying that 10,000 techniques can come from the San Ti Shi Posture.

wu ji posture

Points to remember

1	Your mind must be quiet
2	Your heart must be calm
3	Focus eyes forward
4	Keep your face natural
5	Tip of the tongue in roof of the mouth
6	Clench teeth slightly
7	Relax shoulders, upper chest and hips
8	Breathe from your diaphragm

Stand with your body upright and let the arms hang down naturally by your side. Keep your head erect, your heels together and your toes pointing at 90 degrees to each other.

opening posture

Points to remember

1	**Keep back straight**
2	**Relax shoulders**
3	**Tuck elbows into ribs**
4	**Keep head erect**
5	**Keep knees bent**

From Wu Ji Posture, straighten your left foot, keeping your shoulders relaxed and eyes looking forward. Turn your turn body at the same time so it is at a 45-degree angle. Wuji is stillness, once your body creates movement it becomes Taiji.

Slowly bend your knees with your weight sinking more into your right leg. Bring your left hand up in front of your body and level with your navel, palm down, fingers pointing forward. Bring your right hand over the top of your left hand, palm down and right index finger level with the top of the left middle finger. Keep your eyes looking straight ahead.

san ti shi posture

Step forward with your left leg (two foot-lengths apart) and your left heel in line with your right anklebone. Extend your left hand forward, palm facing out and fingers slightly apart with the middle finger level with your nose. Your palm should be curved as if holding a ball. Bring your right hand level with your navel, palm down and fingers pointing forward. Rest the back edge of your thumb against your navel.

Sink your body weight 60 percent into rear leg and 40 percent into the front leg. Your head should be erect as if being pulled upward, and your eyes should be focused on your left hand. Keep your shoulders and hips relaxed, with the hips and knees gently pulled inward and your feet gripping the floor.

Hold your posture firm and steady, breathing in and out through your nose, and keeping the tip of your tongue in the roof of your mouth. This stance is used in internal martial arts training to build up the body's natural energy. The Chinese call this energy "Qi." Hold the posture for as long as you can before changing to the other side.

Points to remember

1	Back foot 45 degrees
2	Front toe and knee in line (forward)
3	Push with front palm and pull with back palm
4	Until you feel your body tighten inside
5	Breathe naturally
6	Only hold this posture for as long as it is comfortable to you

To check your posture, consider three imaginary vertical lines: Your back should be in line with your rear heel; the elbow of your left arm should be in line with your left knee; and the fingers of your left hand should be in line with your left toes.

The San Ti Shi Posture incorporates the characteristics of four animals; the Legs of the Chicken, the Body of the Dragon, the Shoulders of the Bear and the Head of the Tiger's Embrace.

1. The Legs of a Chicken relate to the weight being mostly on one leg, just as a cockerel in a farmyard struts about then pauses with his weight mostly on one leg.

2. The Body of a Dragon is represented by the body being in three sections, with knees bent and hips slightly bent.

3. The Shoulders of the Bear means that the neck is upright, the head is erect and the eyes are focused forward.

4. The head of the Tiger's Embrace means like a tiger holding its prey.

A circle, represented by the whole palm, relates to Taijiquan. The curved line in the middle of palm relates to Baghua. The straight line between the two dots relates to Xingyiquan.

xingyiquan fist

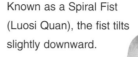

Known as a Spiral Fist
(Luosi Quan), the fist tilts
slightly downward.

The Xingyi fist is unique. The
fist is clenched as normal,
with the thumb pressed on
the mid segment of the middle and index fingers. The
index finger protrudes slightly
forward.

Tiger's mouth

Palm heart

Xingyi Palm (Zhang)

All four fingers are slightly separated with
the index finger pulled up and the thumb
spread out. The other three fingers are
slightly bent and the palm is curved, as if
holding a ball.

xingyiquan stances (bu xing)

These stances are the same as the Tan Tui, but are the higher version.

Points to remember

1	Front knee should not surpass front toe
2	Back leg should not bend at knee
3	Do not lift heel of back leg
4	Toes of back foot should point at 45 degrees
5	Hips and buttocks must not protrude

forward bow stance (gong bu)

The stance is made placing 60 percent weight on the front leg and 40 percent weight on the back leg. This posture is used in Advancing Step.

empty stance (xu bu)

The stance is made
placing 80 percent
weight on the back
leg, 20 percent
weight on the front
leg. The back foot
should be at
45 degrees.

Points to remember

1	Do not lean forward
2	Front heel must not touch floor
3	Hips should not protrude

crouch stance (pu bu)

In a low stance the majority of your weight is on the bent leg. Keep both heels on the floor, with the toes slightly turned out.

Points to remember

1	Do not bend knee of extended leg
2	The heel or outer edge of squatting foot should stay down
3	Outer edge of extended foot should be down
4	Do not draw knee of squatting leg in
5	Do not allow toes of extended leg to point outward

half horse riding stance
(ban ma bu)

The stance is made placing 60 percent weight on the back leg and 40 percent weight on the front leg. Keep both feet flat on the floor.

Points to remember

1	**Do not lean forward**
2	**Supporting knee should not surpass toe**
3	**Supporting knee should not be drawn inward**

dragon stance (long xing)

The stance is made placing 60 percent weight on the back leg. The front leg is stretched further forward than in the Tan Tui form. Sit back on your heel.

This posture is the same as Resting Posture in Tan Tui (Xie Bu) but the front leg is stretched further forward, keeping the buttocks on the back calf/heel.

Points to remember

1	Do not lean forward
2	Front leg should not touch back leg
3	Hips and buttocks must not protrude

scissor stance
– high (jian zi gu bu)

This stance is made placing 40 percent of your weight on the front leg. Your body weight is supported on the ball of the foot (heel slightly raised), with 60 percent of your weight on the back leg.

There are many more stances within the Xingyiquan system; we have looked at just the basic stances within the Five Fists Form.

Points to remember

1   Body should not lean forward

2   Back knee should not touch back of front knee

3   Hips and buttocks should not protrude

Xingyiquan footwork - bu fa
advancing step forward with front leg (Jin Bu)

The footwork is advancing step with follow-up step (Jin Bu). Combined with Lift Step/Cockerel Step (Jixing Bu)

1. San Ti Shi posture.

2. The front leg steps forward one pace, maintaining San Ti Shi posture.

3. The rear leg follow-up step one pace, maintaining 60 percent back leg and 40 percent front leg.

The right foot steps out at 45 degrees to the right, the left foot Follow-Up step keeping 60 percent back leg 40 percent front leg. The next movement is step forward with right leg and bring left foot into right ankle, foot not touching the floor (Ji Xing Bu) Lift Step/Cockerel Step.

advancing step (jin bu)

1. From the San Ti Shi Posture, step forward half a pace with the front leg, pointing the front toe at a 45-degree angle to your body.

2. Step forward one pace with the back leg.

3. End in the San Ti Shi Posture, with 60 percent of your weight on the back leg and 40 percent on your front leg.

step back (tui bu)
back leg stepping back

1. Start in the San Ti Shi Posture.

2. Step back half a pace with your back leg.

3. Transfer 60 percent of your weight onto the back leg.

4. Draw the front leg back to return to the San Ti Shi Posture.

front leg stepping back

1. Start in the San Ti Shi Posture.

2. Step back with the front leg, transferring 60 percent of your body weight on to the back leg.

3. Draw the front leg back to return to the San Ti Shi Posture.

follow up step (gen bu)
front leg step up

1. Start in the San Ti Shi Posture.

2. Step forward one pace with the front leg.

3. Step forward half a pace with the back leg. Maintain 60 percent of your body weight on the back leg.

back leg stepping forward

1. Start in the San Ti Shi Posture.

2. Step forward two paces with the rear leg.

3. Follow up with a step from the now-rear leg. Maintain 60 percent weight on the rear leg.

lift step (ji xing bu)

(This is also known as Cockerel Step)

1. Start in the San Ti Shi Posture.

2. Step forward one pace with the front leg.

3. Bring the rear foot parallel with the front ankle bone. Keep the foot raised, not touching the floor.

There are many more stepping footwork techniques in Xingyiquan, but these are the ones used in the Five Elements.

hand movements (shou fa)

pi quan – splitting fist/chopping fist (for 1st form)

1. Stand in the Wu Ji Posture.

2. Step forward with your left foot into the San Ti Shi Posture. Raise your left arm and keep your right hand drawn back against the navel.

3. Circle your left hand down toward your naval and clench both fists (heart of fist up). The little fingers should touch at your navel, so you create a V shape with your fists.

4. Spiral your left fist upward from your heart to your mouth.

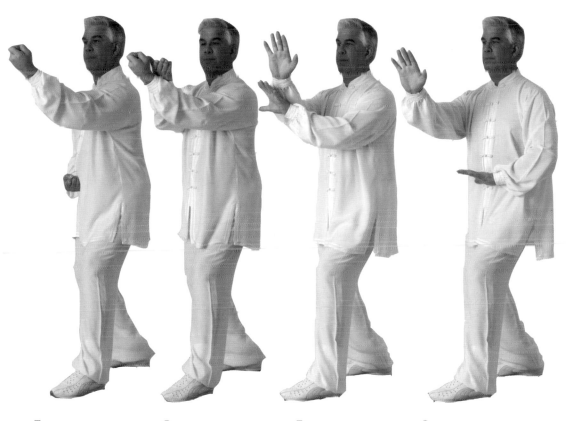

5. Keep your fist in front of your body (nose level with little finger) heart of fist up. Then push the left fist forward.

6. Open your right fist and bring your right palm up to your left hand.

7. Slide the back edge of your right palm along your left forearm. As the palm comes level with the left hand, open the left fist and turn the palm down, in a chopping action.

8. Chop down and forward with the right hand, while pulling the left hand back to your navel. The action you make is as if tearing something apart.

To repeat the movement on the other side:

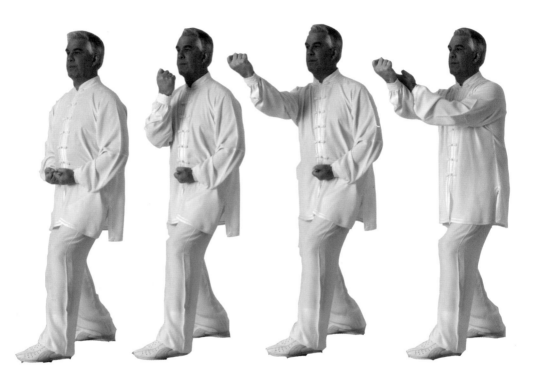

1. Circle your right palm down to your navel, clenching both hands into fists and creating the V shape.

2. Spiral your right fist upward and forward.

3. Take it from your heart to the mouth, in line with your nose.

4. Open your left fist and, with the palm up, slide the back of your left hand along the right forearm, until it reaches the right fist. With right palm open, turn the hand over. Both palms should now be facing down.

Points to remember

1	Hold the San Ti Shi Posture
2	Keep head erect
3	Relax shoulders and hips
4	Breathe naturally with tip of the tongue touching the roof of your mouth
5	Coordinate your hand movements in a smooth transition

5. With the left palm, chop forward and down, while pulling the right palm back to your navel.

6. Pushing your left palm forward and pulling the right palm back is, again, like tearing something in half.

Repeat five times on each side.

chapter 11 the xingyiquan forms

Xingyiquan is characterized by simple and steady movements in very compact routines. A dynamic power is developed through practicing the five basic fists – a power that only comes from regular training and a good coordination of upper and lower limbs, eye, hand, and foot.

The origins of Xingyiquan as a potent fighting art are evident from the rich variety of theoretical and practical self-defense applications the system contains.

The fundamental theory of Xingyiquan is that, when attacked, you absorb your opponent's force and then counter through your opponent's center line in order to repulse his or her attack. In the countering maneuver the power can only be effectively achieved by your whole body arriving at the same point of impact simultaneously.

This focused, but relaxed, training method has many health benefits and is used along side Traditional Chinese Medicine (TCM) for improving the functions of the internal organs and for balancing the energy flow through the heart, stomach, lungs, kidneys and liver.

Students of all ages can gain from these health benefits, and people with chronic health problems can select the particular five-element posture that most helps to increase their state of well-being, enabling the body to start healing.

1st form – splitting fist (pi quan)

hands and feet combined
and jin bu (advancing step)

wu ji posture

Points to remember

1	Keep heels together with toes turned out to 45-degrees (creating a 90-degree angle)
2	Keep arms down by your sides
3	Relax shoulders and hips
4	Keep head erect
5	Focus eyes forward

Start with heels together, toes at a 90-degree angle.

opening posture

Points to remember

1 As you bend your knees, keep your back straight with shoulders and hips relaxed

Turn your left foot so it is facing forward (the right foot does not move). This brings your body to a 45-degree angle. Bend the knees with your body weight sinking more onto the right leg. Circle your left hand up, resting the back of your thumb against your navel. Circle the right hand over the top of the left (middle finger in line with index finger), palms down.

san ti shi posture

Move your left foot forward (two foot lengths). Sinking into the San Ti Shi Posture, push your left hand forward, palm facing out and middle finger level with your nose. Keep the right palm facing down and pulled back.

splitting fist – right side (you pi quan)

2. Spiral the left fist upward and forward, from heart to mouth, and in line with your nose (heart of fist up).

1. Circle your left palm down and, clenching both fists, bring them together at your navel, creating a V shape.

3. At the same time step forward half a pace with your left foot into a forward Bow Stance (Gong Bu) with your toe at an oblique angle (45 degrees outward). Transfer 60 percent body weight onto your front leg. Focus eyes forward.

Points to remember

1	Maintain erect head and body
2	Relax shoulders and hips
3	Make a smooth transition of hands and feet
4	Breathe naturally through the nose
5	Focus eyes forward

4. Step forward into the San Ti Shi Posture. At the same time open the right fist, palm up, and slide it along the left forearm.

5. When the right palm reaches the left hand, open the left fist and turn both palms downward. Create a splitting action, with the right palm chopping forward and the left palm pulling back toward the navel. Make sure your right palm and right foot move and arrive in position at the same time.

splitting fist – left side (zhou pi quan)

1. Circle your right palm down and toward your navel. Clench both fists and bring them together to form a V shape.

2. Spiral your right fist upward and forward, from heart to mouth, with the little finger up.

3. At the same time, step forward half a pace with the right leg, into a forward Bow Stance (Gong Bu). Keep the toes at an oblique angle of 45 degrees. Transfer 60 percent body weight onto your front leg. Focus eyes forward onto the right fist.

4. Open your left fist, palm up, and slide it along the right forearm until it is level with your right fist.

5. Open your right fist and turn both palms downward. Make the splitting movement, with your left palm chopping forward and the right palm pulling back toward your navel. At the same time step forward with your left leg, maintaining 60 percent of your weight on the rear leg. The left palm and left leg should move and arrive in position at the same time.

You can keep practicing these movements going forward (left and right side) three, five, seven, or nine times, depending on the size of your room).

splitting fist – turning movement (zhuan shen pi quan)

You always turn around from the left Splitting Fist Posture (i.e., you make a turn to your right).

1. Clench both fists and bring them together level with your navel, creating a V shape, heart of fist up.

2. At the same time hook your left toe around and turn your body 180 degrees to the right. Raise onto your right toes. You will now be in a left Empty Stance (Xu Bu).

splitting fist – left side (zhou pi quan)

1. Step half a pace forward with right foot into a forward Bow Stance (Gong Bu), with your right toe at a 45-degree angle. Transfer 60 percent of your weight onto your front leg.

2. At the same time spiral your right fist forward and upward (heart to mouth) in front of your body until level with your nose.

3. Open your left fist and turn so the palm faces up. Slide along the right forearm until level with your right fist.

4. Open your right fist and turn both palms down. Chop forward with your left palm while pulling back toward the navel with your right palm. At the same time step forward with the rear leg, maintaining 60 percent weight on your back leg. Left palm and left leg should move together into Splitting Fist.

splitting fist – right side (you pi quan)

1. Clenching both fists, bring both hands together at your navel, creating a V shape.

2. Spiral the left fist upward and forward, from heart to mouth, until level with your nose, heart of fist up.

3. At the same time step forward half a pace with your left foot into a forward Bow Stance (Gong Bu) with toes at a 45-degree angle and 60 percent weight on your front leg. Focus eyes forward.

4. Step forward with right leg (maintaining 60 percent weight on the back leg and 40 percent on front leg) San Ti Shi. At the same time open right fist (palm up) and slide along the left forearm.

5. When your right palm reaches your left fist, open the left fist and turn both palms downward. Chop forward with the right palm while the left palm pulls back toward your navel, creating the splitting action.

Repeat the left and right Splitting Fist, until you come back to your start position.

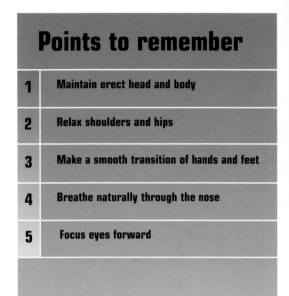

Points to remember

1	Maintain erect head and body
2	Relax shoulders and hips
3	Make a smooth transition of hands and feet
4	Breathe naturally through the nose
5	Focus eyes forward

Left side reminder

splitting fist – turning movement (pi quan hui shen)

You always turn around from the left Splitting Fist Posture (that is, you turn to your right).

1. Bring your left palm in (clenching into fist, creating the V shape—heart of fist up).

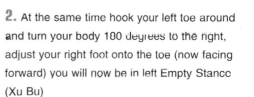

2. At the same time hook your left toe around and turn your body 100 degrees to the right, adjust your right foot onto the toe (now facing forward) you will now be in left Empty Stance (Xu Bu)

splitting fist – left side (zhou pi quan)

Step half a pace forward with your right foot into a forward Bow Stance (Gong Bu), with right toe at a 45-degree angle.

1. Transfer 60 percent of your weight onto your front leg.

2. At the same time spiral your right fist forward and upward in front of your body (heart to mouth) until level with your nose.

3. Open your left fist and turn the palm so it is facing up. Slide it along the right forearm until level with your right fist.

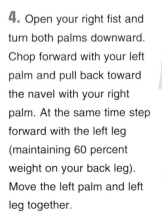

4. Open your right fist and turn both palms downward. Chop forward with your left palm and pull back toward the navel with your right palm. At the same time step forward with the left leg (maintaining 60 percent weight on your back leg). Move the left palm and left leg together.

closing movement (shou shi)

From left Splitting Fist

1. Bring your left foot back to the right foot. Point the left toes forward and the right toes at 45 degrees. Your body should now be 45 degrees to your right (same as your starting position).

2. Finish in Closing Posture – relaxed with arms by your sides. To see how the Splitting Fist (Pi Quan) corresponds to the Five Elements, refer to the chart on pages 156–157.

2nd form – crushing fist (beng quan) – (wood)

fist work only

1. Start in a left Ti Shi Posture.

2. Clench fists and, keeping the right fist forward, rotate the left fist back toward your navel.

3. While rotating the right fist backward, punch out with the left arm, between waist and shoulder height, eye of fist up.

4. Keep the fist at a slight angle downward (Spiral Fist).

5. Repeat the punch with your right fist. Rotate the left fist back to your navel, and rotate the right fist forward, eye of fist up, with the fist at a slight angle downward. Repeat ten times.

Points to remember

1	Maintain the San Ti Shi posture
2	Coordinate your punching movement
3	Generate your punch from your waist
4	Keep your posture erect
5	Breathe naturally

Then change to a right San Ti Shi Posture and repeat the Crushing Fist Exercise.

crushing fist (beng quan)
hands and feet combined together

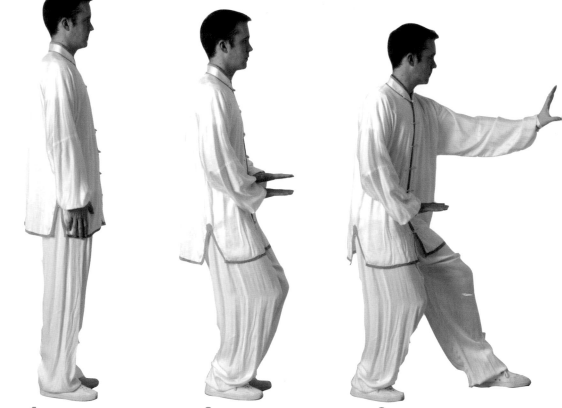

1. Start in the Wu Ji Posture.

2. Turn your left foot to face forward, bringing your body to a 45-degree angle. Bend your knees, sinking your weight onto your right leg. Raise the left hand and then the right so that the backs of your thumbs rest against your navel, palms facing down.

3. Step forward with your left foot into the San Ti Shi Posture. Push your left palm forward and keep your right hand back against the navel.

right crushing fist (you beng quan)

1. Clench both fists and step forward one pace with your left leg into a forward Bow Stance (Gong Bu).

2. At the same time draw your left fist back to your navel.

3. Punch forward rotating your right fist, eye of the fist up, and step up half a pace with the back leg.

left crushing fist (zhou beng quan)

1. Clench both fists and step forward one pace with your left leg into a forward Bow Stance (Gong Bu).

2. At the same time draw your right fist back to your navel.

3. Punch forward rotating your left fist, eye of fist up, and follow up half a pace with the back leg.

You can repeat these moves as many times as you like depending on the size of the area you are training in.

Right side reminder

turning movement (beng quan)

1. Stand with your left foot and right fist forward (right Crushing Fist). Draw the right fist back to your navel and level with the left fist, to create a V shape.

2. Hook your left toe around and transfer the weight onto your left leg as you turn your body 180 degrees to the right. Raise the right foot on toes—Empty Step (Xu Bu). Keep your body weight on the rear leg.

3. Raise your right knee up above hip height and spiral the right fist forward and upward to chin level, heart of fist up.

4. Kick your right foot forward and heel kick (Deng Tui) with the ankle flexed, pushing power into the heel. Kick up to waist height.

5. Drop forward onto the front foot (Crushing Kick—Cai Jiao) at a 45-degree angle. Follow up with a step from the back leg, so that the knee touches the hollow at the back of the knee of the front leg. At the same time apply the left Splitting Fist. You should be in Scissor Posture (Jian Zi Gu Bu) with right foot forward at an oblique angle. Left palm should face forward, while right palm pulls back at the navel.

right crushing fist (you beng quan)

1. Step forward one pace with your left leg, and punch forward with a rotating right fist.

2. Bring the left fist back to the navel.

3. Follow up with a half step from the back leg, maintaining the San Ti Shi Posture.

left crushing fist (zhou beng quan)

1. Clench both fists and step forward one pace with the left leg.

2. At the same time draw the right fist back to your navel.

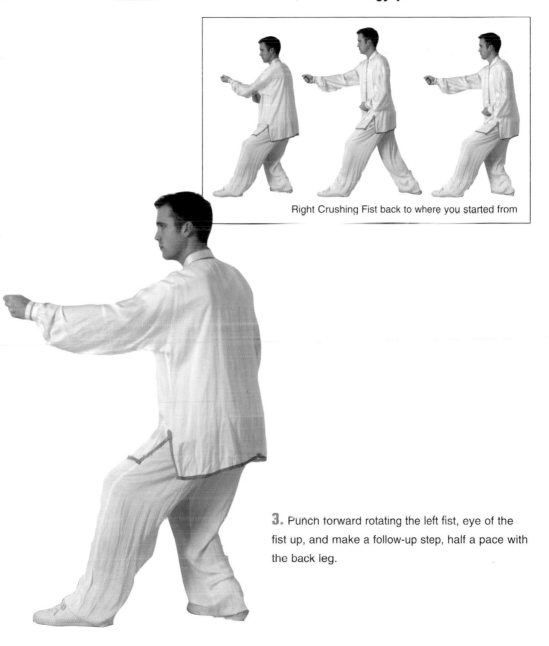

Right Crushing Fist back to where you started from

3. Punch forward rotating the left fist, eye of the fist up, and make a follow-up step, half a pace with the back leg.

turning movement

1. Stand with the left foot and right fist forward (right Crushing Fist). Draw your right fist back to the navel, level with the left fist, to create a V shape.

2. Hook the left toe around, transferring the weight to the left leg and turn your body 180 degrees to your right. Raise the right foot up on toes—Empty Step (Xu Bu). Keep your body weight on the rear leg.

3. Raise your right knee up above hip height and spiral the right fist forward and upward to chin level, heart of fist up.

4. Kick your right foot forward, heel kick (Deng Tui) with the ankle flexed, pushing power into the heel. Kick up to waist height.

6. Step forward one pace with your left leg.

5. Drop forward onto the front foot (Crushing Kick—Cai Jiao) at a 45-degree angle, and follow up with a step from the back leg, so that the knee touches the hollow at the back of the knee of the front leg. At the same time apply the left Splitting Fist. You should be in Scissor Posture (Jian Zi Gu Bu), with the right foot forward at an oblique angle. The left palm should face forward, with the right palm pulled back to navel.

7. Punch forward with a rotating right fist.

8. Bring your left fist back to the navel and make a half step with the back leg, back to San Ti Shi Posture.

Points to remember

1	It is important to hold the San Ti Shi Posture (60 percent back leg 40 percent front leg) while doing follow up step
2	Coordinate punch with footwork
3	Punch using whole body, don't raise your shoulders
4	Keep back straight and head erect
5	Always focus eyes on front fist
6	Breathe naturally

closing movement

To see how Beng Quan (Crushing Fist) corresponds to the Elements, refer to the Five Element chart on pages 156–157.

1. Stand in left San Ti Shi Posture with right fist forward (Crushing Fist).

2. Bring the left heel back to the right heel, left toe pointing forward, and right toe at a 45-degree angle. Bring your right fist back to the left fist and drop both arms down by your sides.

3rd form – drilling fist (zuan quan) – water

fist only (shou fa)

left fist

1. Start in the Wu Ji Posture.

2. Step forward with your left foot, left palm forward, into the San Ti Shi Posture.

3. Holding the San Ti Shi Posture, clench both fists. Rotate your left fist, heart down, and right fist, heart up.

4. Punch forward, drilling upward from heart to mouth, with the right fist between chin and eye level.

5. Press down with the left fist until it comes under the right forearm.

right fist

1. Repeat on the other side. Rotate right fist downward.

2. Drill left fist forward and up from heart to mouth until between chin and eye level.

3. Press down with the right fist until it comes under the left forearm.

Change your San Ti Shi Posture from left to right.

drilling fist (zuan quan)
hands & feet combined together
with advanced step (jin bu) and
follow-up step (gen bu)

1. Start in the Wu Ji posture.

2. Turn your left foot to face forward, bringing your body to a 45-degree angle. Bend your knees, sinking your weight onto your right leg. Raise the left hand and then the right so that the backs of your thumbs rest against your navel, palms facing down.

3. Stand in left San Ti Shi, with the left palm forward and the right palm back.

right drilling fist (you zuan quan)

1 Clench both fists. Rotate the left fist, pressing downward, and the right fist drilling up from heart to mouth, until between chin and eye level.

2. Move the left foot half a pace forward, with toes at a 45-degree angle. Sweep the left fist under the right forearm. At the same time step forward one pace with the rear foot.

3. With a half-pace follow-up step with left foot, finish the move with your right foot and right fist forward and 60 percent weight on the back leg.

left drilling fist (zhou zuan quan)

1. Rotate the right fist downward and drill the left fist up, from heart to mouth, until between chin and eye level. Move the right foot half a pace forward with toes at a 45-degree angle.

2. Rotate the right fist under the left forearm. At same time step forward one pace with the rear foot and make a half-pace follow-up step with the right foot.

3. Finish with the left foot and left fist forward, and with 60 percent weight on your back leg and 40 percent on your front leg.

turning movement.

1. From the left drilling fist, turn your body to the right, by hooking the left toe around.

2. Transfer your weight onto the left leg with the right toe touching the floor – Empty Stance (Xu Bu). Keep the left fist out in front of your body and the right fist under the left forearm.

3. Step forward with the right foot, pointing the toes at a 45-degree angle.

4. Rotate the left fist down and drill the right fist up.

5. Rotate the right fist down and drill the left fist up. At the same time step forward one pace with the rear leg, with the left fist and left leg forward.

6. Step up half a pace with the rear leg. Repeat the left and right Drilling Fist the same number of times until you return to your starting position.

turning movement

1. From the left drilling fist, turn your body to the right, by hooking the left toe around.

2. Transfer your weight onto the left leg with the right toe touching the floor—Empty Stance (Xu Bu). Keep the left fist out in front of your body and the right fist under your left forearm.

3. Step forward with your right foot, toes pointing at 45 degrees. Rotate the left fist down and drill the right fist up.

closing movement (shou shi)

2. Right Drilling fist forward, and right foot forward.

3. Bring the front foot back to the right heel.

1. Rotate the right fist down while drilling the left fist up. Step forward with the left leg, at the same time and make a follow-up step with right leg. Keep 60 percent weight on your back leg and 40 percent on your front leg.

4. Let your arms hang down by your sides.

To see how Drilling Fist corresponds to the Five Elements, refer to chart on pages 156–157.

4th form – cannon fist (pao quan) – Fire

fist movement only

1. Start in the Wu Ji Posture.

2. Move into a left San Ti Shi Posture.

3. Clench both fists and circle down toward the navel.

4. Join the fists to create a V shape at the navel, heart of fist up.

5. Circle the left fist up across your body to the side of your forehead. At the same time turn your body 45 degrees to the left.

6. Punch forward with your right fist at chest height, eye of fist up.

7. Bring the left fist down level with the right fist.

8. Circle both fists down to your navel to create a V shape. Turn your body to face forward.

9. Circle the right fist up across the center line of your body, to the side of your forehead. Keep shoulders and elbow relaxed, eye of fist downward and heart of fist outward.

Points to remember

1	Hold the San Ti Shi Posture and practice both sides
2	Keep shoulders and elbows relaxed
3	Coordinate block and punch at the same time
4	Keep back straight and head erect
5	Focus eyes toward front fist
6	Breathe naturally

10. Turn your body 45 degrees to the right and punch forward with the left fist chest level, eye of fist up.

cannon fist (pao quan) hands and feet combined

advanced step (jin bu), follow-up step (gen bu) and cockerel step (ji xing bu)

1. Start in the Wu Ji Posture.

2. Turn your left foot to face forward, bringing your body to a 45-degree angle. Bend your knees, sinking your weight onto your right leg. Raise the left hand and then the right so that the backs of your thumbs rest against your navel, palms facing down.

3. Stand in a left San Ti Shi Posture.

cannon fist – left side (zhou pao quan)

1. Step forward half a pace with the front leg, into the Bow Stance (Gong Bu). Bring the right leg in line with the left palm. Step through two paces with the rear leg.

2. Bring the left foot level with the right ankle and raise onto the toes. Circle the palms down to the navel, clenching both fists.

3. Maintaining your balance, turn your body 45 degrees to the left. Circle the left fist up and across the center line of your body. Step out one pace with the left leg at a 45-degree angle.

4. Follow up with a step from the rear leg, keeping 60 percent of your weight on the rear leg. Continue to circle the left fist up to the side of your forehead, while punching forward with your right fist at chest level.

cannon fist – right side (you pao quan)

Points to remember

1	**Keep your block and punch coordinated**
2	**Keep a 45-degree angle with block and punch**
3	**Maintain your balance on the lift step**
4	**Keep shoulders and hips relaxed**
5	**Focus your eyes to the front fist**

1. Step forward one pace with your left foot. Circle the left fist down to the right fist and circle in an arc down to your navel. Create a V shape with your fists.

2. Bring the right foot in level with the left ankle and raise onto the toes.

3. Circle the right fist up to the side of your forehead.

4. Punch at 45 degrees with the right fist, keeping the left fist at chest height, eye of fist up. At the same time step forward one pace with the right foot at a 45-degree angle and follow up with a step from the left foot, maintaining the weight distribution of 60–40 percent.

turning movement

1. From right Pao Quan, rotate your fists so that heart of fist is up, and the left fist is at chest height, with the right at temple height.

2. Hook the right foot around and turn your body to the left by 90 degrees.

3. Transfer your weight onto the right foot and bring the left foot into the lift step.

4. Circle your fists down to the navel, heart of fist up.

Repeat Left and Right side Pao Quan, back to your starting position.

turning movement

1. From right Pao Quan, rotate your fists, heart of fist up, so that the left fist is at chest height and the right fist is at temple height.

2. Hook the right foot around and turn your body to the left by 90-degrees.

3. Transfer your weight onto the right foot, and bring the left foot into a lift step.

4. Circle your fists down to the navel, heart of fist up.

left pao quan

1. Clench your fists and circle the left fist up to the side of your forehead. Punch forward with the right fist at chest height, eye of fist up. At the same time step forward one pace to the left with your left foot and at a 45-degree angle.

2. Follow up with a step from the right foot maintaining 60 percent body weight on the back leg and 40 percent on the front leg.

Points to remember

1 The block upward is a defensive move and the punch is a counterattack

To see how the Cannon Fist corresponds to the Five Elements, refer to the chart on pages 156–157.

closing movement (shou shi)

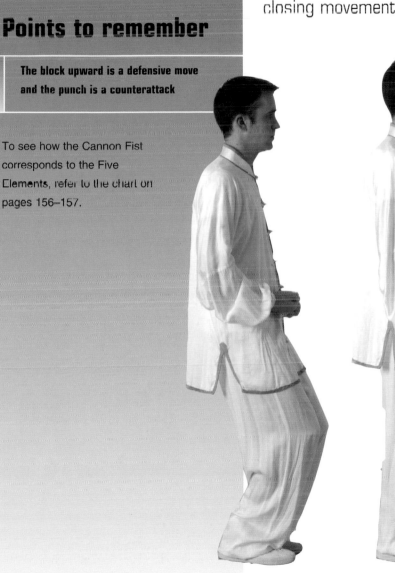

1. Change the back foot from a 45-degree to a 90-degree angle, and bring the left foot level with the right.

2. Relax your arms down by your sides, with your eyes looking forward.

5th form – crossing/swing punch - heng quan – Earth

hand movement only (shou fa)

left side

1. Stand in the Wu Ji Posture.

2. Move into a left San Ti Shi Posture.

3. Clench both fists and circle the right fist under the left forearm.

4. Continue the movement up to your left, at a 45-degree angle, heart of fist up, until between waist and shoulder level.

5. Circle your left fist down to your navel, heart of fist down.

6. Turn your body 90 degrees to your right.

7. Rotate your left fist up and forward to your right, under your right forearm, heart up, until between waist and shoulder level.

8. Circle your right fist down toward the navel, heart of fist down.

right side

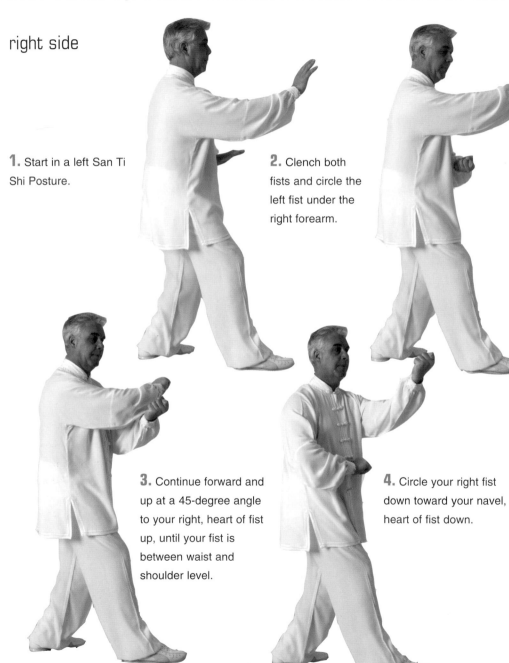

1. Start in a left San Ti Shi Posture.

2. Clench both fists and circle the left fist under the right forearm.

3. Continue forward and up at a 45-degree angle to your right, heart of fist up, until your fist is between waist and shoulder level.

4. Circle your right fist down toward your navel, heart of fist down.

5. Turn your body 90 degrees to your left.

6. Rotate your right fist upward and forward to your left, under your left forearm, right fist heart up, until between waist and shoulder level.

7. Right fist circle downward toward navel, heart of fist down.

Repeat Crossing Fist on both left and right sides.

crossing/swing punch (heng quan)
hands and feet combined together

advanced step (jin bu), follow-up step (gen bu) and cockerel step (ji xing bu)

1. Start in the Wu Ji Posture.

2. Turn your left foot to face forward, bringing your body to a 45-degree angle. Bend your knees, sinking your weight onto your right leg. Raise the left hand and then the right so that the backs of your thumbs rest against your navel, palms facing down.

3. Step into a left San Ti Shi Posture.

right crossing fist (you heng quan)

1. Turn your body 45 degrees to the left. Clench both fists, then circle your left fist down to your navel, heart of fist down.

2. Rotate the right fist upward and forward, heart of fist up, and at a 45-degree angle to your left fist. At the same time follow up with one pace forward with the left leg, at a 45-degree angle.

3. Step forward with the left foot one pace, and bring the right foot up level with the left ankle, but not touching the floor. Keep your body weight on the left leg (Cockerel Step) and keep your fists in the same position.

left crossing fist (zhou heng quan)

1. Turn your body 45 degrees to the right. Clench both fists, then circle the right fist down to your navel, heart of fist down. Rotate the left fist upward and forward, heart of fist up, and at 45 degrees to your right.

2. At the same time, follow up one pace forward with your right leg, 45 degrees to the right.

3. Step forward one pace with your right foot, and bring the left foot up level with the right ankle, but not touching the floor. Keep your body weight on your right leg (Cockerel Step) and keep fists in same position. Body facing forward.

Repeat Crossing Fist on both your left and right sides.

turning movement

1. In left Heng Quan, stand with right foot and left fist forward.

2. Turn your body to the left, hooking the right foot around by 90 degrees.

3. Transfer your weight onto the right leg and bring your left foot level with the right ankle (Cockerel Step). Keep your arms in the same position.

4. Circle your right fist under the left forearm, rotating upward and forward, heart of fist up, to between waist and shoulder level. Follow up with a 45-degree angle with your left foot.

5. Circle your left fist downward to the navel, heart of fist down.

Repeat Crossing Fist on both left and right sides until you return to your starting position.

turning movement.

1. In right Heng Quan, stand with your right foot and left fist forward.

2. Turn your body to the left, hooking the right foot around 90 degrees. Transfer your weight onto the right leg and bring the left foot into the right ankle.

3. Keep your arms in the same position and your body weight on the right leg.

4. Follow up with a step with the left foot at 45-degree angle.

5. Circle your right fist under the left forearm rotating upward and forward, heart of fist up, until between waist and shoulder level.

6. Circle your left fist down toward the navel, heart of fist down.

closing movement

Points to remember

1	**Correct posture**
2	**Coordination between upper and lower limbs**
3	**In Cockerel Step maintain weight on one leg**
4	**Train your balance**
5	**Take each movement step by step**

1. From right Heng Quan, stand with the left foot and right fist forward. Turn the right foot from 45 degrees to 90 degrees and bring the left heel into the right heel.

2. Relax your arms, letting them hang down by your sides.

To see how Crossing Fist corresponds to the Elements, refer to the Five Element chart on pages 156–157.

The five basic fists of Xingyiquan can be used in many different ways for self-defense. They are simple techniques but can be very effective.

In "internal" martial arts' self-defense has a different theory from that in "external" martial arts.

When the attacker moves forward to initiate an attack in the "external" art, you block counter as hard as you can.

With the "internal," arts you absorb the attack, then you divert the force to upset the attacker's balance. Then you counterattack back to a weakened attack.

splitting fist (pi quan)

From an attacker punching to the body.

1. The attack.

2. Get into the San Ti Shi Posture. As the punch comes in, chop down with your left and right palms onto the attacker's forearm and shoulder, using enough pressure to affect your attacker's balance.

3. Step half a pace forward with a follow-up step, circling your palm upward and forward from heart to mouth.

4. Apply a double-palm strike to your attacker's head and heart.

crushing fist (beng quan)

From an attack from a low kick and a punch to the face. The defense is from the turning movement of Heel Kick (deng tui) and Crushing Kick (Cia Jiao).

1. Get into the Knee Raise Posture as your attacker moves to kick. Kick downward with a heel to the attacker's knee.

2. As the attacker moves to punch your face, apply Splitting Fist onto the wrist and elbow, pressing downward. Keep your foot on the attacker's knee.

3. Drop your body weight down onto your attacker's arm and leg, forcing him to the floor.

drilling fist (zuan quan)

From an attacker gripping your wrist.

1. Get into the San Ti Shi Posture, as the attacker grips your wrist.

2. Circle one of the gripped wrists in a downward motion clenching your fist. The circle should be big enough to break your attacker's balance.

3. As you draw your arm down, your attacker's head will be drawn forward.

4. Drill up and forward with your other fist, heart of fist up, under your attacker's chin.

cannon fist (pao quan)

From a hook punch or kick to the head.

1. Get into the San Ti Shi Posture as the punch or kick hooks around toward your head. Step at a 45-degree angle with your front leg and gain the same momentum as the attack.

2. Circle your nearest arm upward and outward to deflect the punch or kick, then punch forward into attacker's chest moving through his center line.

crossing fist (heng quan)

From an attacker performing an uppercut.

1. Get into the San Ti Shi Posture as the attacker uppercuts. Step 45 degrees to the outside of the attacker's arm, to bring your attacker off balance.

2. Deflect the grip with your front arm. Step forward with the front left foot. Circle your other fist under your front arm and punch into your attacker's body (Hidden Punch).

afterword

This book has been written to give you, the reader, a brief insight into the vast subject of Kung Fu/Wushu. Even after forty years of training, teaching and studying, I have only travelled a short journey down the long path of Chinese martial arts.

As is quite often the case, especially in books of this nature, certain discrepancies may appear in the main body of text. Any such discrepancies that you may find are the responsibility of me, the author, and should in no way reflect upon the teachers/mentors named on page 256.

bibliography

A Guide to Chinese Martial Arts
By Li Tianji & Du Xilian
Foreign Languages Press, Beijing, China.

Northern Shaolin
Twelve Tantui Boxing Series
Editor: Chan Kin Man
Chan Hong Heung Kung Fu Association, Hong Kong.

Xing Yi Quan Xue
The Study of Form-Mind Boxing
By Sun Lu Tang
High View Publications, USA.

Li Tianji's
The Skill of Xingyiquan
By Li Tianji
TGL Books, Canada.

index

credits & acknowledgements

I would like to acknowledge the following Masters for their kindness, patience and prowess in passing on their skills and their Chinese heritage.

Without these very special mentors I would never have started or continued my journey of Kung Fu/Wushu, which has completely changed my life.

My respects to my late father-in-law, Chee Soo (Clifford Chee Soo)

My special respects to the late Master Huang Jifu, who dramatically enhanced my career in Chinese martial arts.

To Grandmaster Chen Yuhe (Tan Geok Ho), for his inspiration, and boundless energy.

To Professor Li Deyin, for his scientific and technical coaching.

I would like to thank all those who have helped me with this book, for their ideas and encouragement.

I would like to thank my son Jason for his invaluable help and my daughter Berdita for her assistance.

Last but not least to my wife for all her help.

The author and publishers would also like to thank Peter's students, Edward Gomersall and Elaine Koster, for appearing in the book.